DRAGON'S LAIR ADVENTURE

A Step-by-Step GUIDE

to Creating a Text-Based Game in PYTHON

using ChatGPT

by SIMON KIM

LAIAN DANA

DRAGON'S LAIR ADVENTURE

A Step-by-Step Guide
to Creating a Text-Based Game
in Python using ChatGPT

By Simon Kim

Table of Contents

INTRODUCTION

Embark on a thrilling adventure with Dragon's Lair! This comprehensive guide takes you through the journey of creating a text-based game using Python programming. Follow the hero as they face challenges, defeat monsters, and collect treasure on their quest to save a kingdom from a powerful dragon.

In this book, you'll learn the basics of Python programming and how to apply it to game design and development. Discover the secrets to creating an engaging story plot, memorable characters, and dynamic combat mechanics.

Leverage the power of OpenAI ChatGPT[1] to enhance your game-making skills and take your programming to the next level. Whether you're a beginner or an experienced developer, this book provides all the knowledge and tools needed to bring your own text-based game to life. So grab your notebook and join us on this exciting journey in the world of Dragon's Lair Adventure.

IMPORTANT: This book is aimed at beginners who are new to Python programming, but it is assumed that the reader has prior knowledge of a Python IDE such as Visual Studio Code or Google Colab. For those who have some experience with these IDEs and just need a reference for reminder, the information on how to install and set them up can be found in the appendix section. If you are completely new to Python IDEs, we recommend that you familiarize yourself with one before diving into this book. This will help ensure that you get the most out of the book and are able to follow along with the examples and exercises.

---

[1] OpenAI ChatGPT: OpenAI ChatGPT is a language generation model developed by OpenAI, designed to generate human-like text based on a given prompt. This model is trained on a large corpus of text data, allowing it to generate coherent and contextually relevant responses to various types of prompts. In this book, we will be using OpenAI ChatGPT to help us create a text-based game, by using its natural language processing capabilities to add depth and complexity to the game's story and characters.

Preface

Welcome to Dragon's Lair Adventure, a text-based game that will take you on a thrilling journey through a kingdom threatened by a powerful dragon. This game is designed to challenge your problem-solving skills, test your combat abilities, and immerse you in a world of fantasy and adventure.

This book is a guide to playing Dragon's Lair Adventure. It will provide you with all the information you need to start playing, including the game's plot, mechanics, and controls. It will also give you tips and strategies for defeating the dragon and saving the kingdom.

We have worked hard to make this game as engaging and enjoyable as possible. We hope that you will enjoy playing it as much as we enjoyed creating it. Thank you for choosing Dragon's Lair Adventure and happy gaming!

Sincerely, Simon Kim with the help of OpenAI's ChatGPT.

Chapter 1: Setting the Stage
- The Kingdom in Danger

Created using Midjourney

The kingdom is in peril. A powerful dragon has been terrorizing the land, burning villages and killing innocent people. The king and his army have tried to defeat the dragon, but to no avail. It seems that the dragon is invincible.

The people of the kingdom are desperate for a hero to rise up and save them. That hero is you. You are a brave warrior, mage, or rogue, and you have been chosen to embark on a quest to defeat the dragon and save the kingdom.

You will begin your journey in a forest, where you will encounter various obstacles such as traps and puzzles. You will also have to fight off goblins and other monsters. As you progress through the forest, you will come across treasure and items that will help you on your quest.

But the forest is just the beginning. You will soon find yourself on a mountain, home to trolls and other powerful monsters. You will have to use your skills and weapons to defeat them, and you will also have to navigate through treacherous terrain and solve puzzles to progress.

Finally, you will reach the dragon's lair. Here, you will have to use all of your skills and abilities to defeat the dragon. The battle will be challenging, and you will have to use strategy and planning to emerge victorious.

Will you rise to the challenge and save the kingdom? The fate of the kingdom is in your hands.

1.1 Install Python IDE

Created using Midjourney

Many beginner programmers face difficulties when installing and setting up a Python IDE, especially those who are new to programming or have limited experience with computers. However, this should not stop you from learning Python programming.

In order to help you overcome this initial challenge, we have provided comprehensive information and step-by-step instructions in Appendix A.1. By following these instructions, you will be able to set up your IDE with ease and start coding right away. So, let's embrace this challenge and move forward in our journey towards learning Python programming.

TIPS with ChatGPT to Get Help on Setting Up Your Python IDE:

If you are still struggling with figuring out which Python IDE to use or have difficulties setting it up, you can always resort to the live chatbot, ChatGPT, for more assistance. Simply start by typing "Hey ChatGPT, please give me more detailed instructions on setting up a Python IDE." ChatGPT can provide you with step-by-step instructions and answer any questions you may have about setting up your Python environment. Whether you choose to work with Visual Studio Code or Google Colab, ChatGPT is always there to help you get started and make the most out of your programming experience.

1.2 Getting to Know Jupyter Notebook: A Beginner's Guide

Created using Midjourney

We suggest that you begin your Python journey by working with Jupyter Notebook in either Visual Studio Code or Google Colab, unless you are already familiar with working with `*.py` files. Later on, you will be introduced to working with `*.py` files. Jupyter Notebook is an open-source web application that allows you to create and share documents that contain live code, equations, visualizations, and narrative text. It is widely used for data science and machine learning tasks, as well as for general coding and scripting.

To get started with Jupyter Notebook on Visual Studio Code, you will need to have Visual Studio Code installed on your computer. Once you have it installed, follow these steps to set up Jupyter Notebook:

- Open Visual Studio Code and click on the Extensions icon (represented by a square with a dot in the center) on the left-side panel.
- In the search bar, type "Jupyter" and select the "Jupyter" extension by Microsoft.
- Click the Install button to install the Jupyter extension.
- After the installation is complete, click the Reload button to activate the extension.
- With the Jupyter extension installed and activated, you can now create a Jupyter Notebook file by clicking on the File menu and selecting New Notebook.

Note: If you prefer to work with Jupyter Notebook in a web browser, you can use Google Colab instead. With Google Colab, you will be directly led to a Jupyter environment, where you can start coding and working with Jupyter Notebook.

When you launch Jupyter Notebook, you will be taken to the dashboard where you can create a new notebook or open an existing one. A Jupyter Notebook consists of cells, which can contain text, code, or other types of content. You can run the code in a cell by pressing `Shift + Enter` or by clicking the `Run` button in the toolbar.

Jupyter Notebook also provides many useful features, such as code completion, syntax highlighting, and interactive widgets, that can make coding and exploring data much easier. It's a great tool for anyone looking to learn Python or for those who need to perform data analysis tasks.

Here are some tips to troubleshoot Jupyter Notebook errors with the help of ChatGPT:

Get specific: When reaching out to ChatGPT, be specific about the error you are encountering. This will help ChatGPT to provide you with a more targeted solution.

Provide context: Explain the steps you took before encountering the error, as well as the environment you are working in (e.g. Jupyter Notebook on Visual Studio Code or Google Colab).

Check for updates: Make sure your Jupyter Notebook is up to date. If you are using Visual Studio Code, check for updates to the Python extension. If you are using Google Colab, check for updates to the Jupyter Notebook environment.

Search the web: Before reaching out to ChatGPT, try searching for the error you are encountering. There may already be a solution available on the web.

Test your code: Try running your code in a different environment to see if the error persists. This can help you determine if the error is specific to Jupyter Notebook or if it is a more general issue with your code.

By following these tips, you can effectively troubleshoot Jupyter Notebook errors with the help of ChatGPT.

1.3 Introduction to the kingdom and the threat posed by the dragon

Created using Midjourney

With your Python IDE installed and ready to go, it's time to dive into coding. To get started, let's utilize the `print` function to print out the narrative of the adventure story. In Python, you use the `print` function by placing your message within the parentheses as follows. Herein, the symbol ` is located on the tilde key, not the quotation key.

```
print("This is the example of the `print` function")
```

The following is an example of the code to introduce the adventure story:

```python
def introduction():
    print("You are a brave adventurer living in a kingdom under
threat from a powerful dragon.")
    print("The dragon has been terrorizing the kingdom, destroying
villages and hoarding treasure.")
    print("The people of the kingdom are in dire need of a hero to
defeat the dragon and restore peace.")
    print("You have decided to take on this dangerous quest and
become that hero.")
    print("Your journey begins now...")

if __name__ == "__main__":
    introduction()
```

The code defines a function called "introduction" that outputs a series of messages to the console. The function uses the "print" statement to display the messages, which describe the background and context of the game. The messages present the player as a brave adventurer who has taken on a quest to defeat a dragon that is terrorizing the kingdom.

A function in Python is a block of code that performs a specific task. Functions help break our program into smaller and modular chunks. As our program grows larger and more complex, functions make it more organized and manageable. Functions also allow us to reuse code across our program, which makes it easier to develop and maintain. In Python, functions are defined using the `def` keyword followed by the function name and a set of parentheses that may include parameters. The code within the function is indented and is executed when the function is called. Functions can return a value using the return keyword.

The code also includes an `if __name__ == "__main__":` statement. This is a common pattern in Python that is used to determine if the code is being run as a standalone script or being imported as a module into another script. In this case, the code is checking if the script is being run as a standalone script and if so, it calls the "introduction" function. The purpose of this is to ensure that the function is only run when the script is executed and not when it is imported as a module into another script.

Consult ChatGPT for information regarding indentation in Python programming!

Indentation is a key feature of the Python programming language. In Python, indentation is used to define blocks of code, such as functions, loops, and conditionals. The amount of indentation is significant and determines the structure of the code. A block of code must be indented the same number of spaces for all of its lines, and the same number of spaces for each line within the block. This makes it easy to visually see the structure of the code and helps to avoid syntax errors. Indentation is also used to indicate the end of a block of code, so that the Python interpreter knows when to exit that block. Proper indentation is crucial to writing clean, readable, and efficient code in Python.

Here is an example of indentation in Python:

```python
def greet(name):
  if name == "John":
    print("Hello, John!")
  else:
    print("Hello, stranger!")

greet("John")
greet("Jane")
```

In this example, the if statement and the else statement are indented by four spaces to indicate that they are part of the greet function. The same indentation is used for the print statements within each condition. This is a common convention in Python and helps to visually distinguish the structure of the code.

1.4 Display of the main menu with options for the player to start the game or quit

Created using Midjourney

Upon starting the game, the player will be presented with the main menu. The main menu will display options for the player to either start the game or quit. This is an important part of the game as it sets the stage for the player's journey and allows them to make a choice before beginning.

```python
def main_menu():
    print("Welcome to Dragon's Lair Adventure!")
    print("1. Start game")
    print("2. Quit")
    menu_choice = int(input("Enter your choice: "))
    if menu_choice == 1:
        start_game()
    elif menu_choice == 2:
        quit_game()
    else:
        print("Invalid choice. Please enter 1 or 2.")
        main_menu()

def start_game():
    print("You are a brave adventurer on a quest to defeat the dragon
```

```
and save the kingdom.")
    # continue game progression


def quit_game():
    print("Thank you for playing Dragon's Lair Adventure. Goodbye!")
    # end game


if __name__ == "__main__":
    main_menu()
```

In this code, the `main_menu` function is defined to display the options for the player to start the game or quit. The player's choice is taken as input and stored in the variable `menu_choice`. If the player chooses 1, the `start_game` function is called. If the player chooses 2, the `quit_game` function is called. If the player enters an invalid option, an error message is displayed and the `main_menu` function is called again. The `start_game` and `quit_game` functions are left blank for now and will be developed in later chapters. You will notice that the symbol "#" is used for commenting out in Python.

By using this code, the player will be able to make a choice at the beginning of the game and start their journey.

Get Help with `if` Clauses: Ask ChatGPT for More Details on the `if` Statement!

The `if` statement in Python is used for conditional execution of code. It allows you to execute a block of code only if a specified condition is met. The syntax of the if statement is as follows:

```
if condition:
    # execute this code block if condition is True
```

Here, condition is any expression that can be evaluated as either True or False. If the condition is True, the code block indented under the if statement will be executed. If the condition is False, the code block will be skipped.

For example:

```
x = 5

if x > 3:
    print("x is greater than 3")
```

In this example, x is assigned the value of 5, and the condition x > 3 is True, so the code block under the if statement will be executed and the message "x is greater than 3" will be printed to the console.

You can also use the else clause with the if statement to specify what to do if the condition is False. The syntax is as follows:

```
if condition:
    # execute this code block if condition is True
else:
    # execute this code block if condition is False
```

For example:

```
x = 2

if x > 3:
    print("x is greater than 3")
else:
    print("x is not greater than 3")
```

In this example, x is assigned the value of 2, and the condition x > 3 is False, so the code block under the else clause will be executed and the message "x is not greater than 3" will be printed to the console.

You can also use the elif clause to specify multiple conditions and associated code blocks. The syntax is as follows:

```
if condition1:
    # execute this code block if condition1 is True
elif condition2:
    # execute this code block if condition1 is False and condition2
is True
```

```
else:
    # execute this code block if both condition1 and condition2 are
False
```

In this example, the conditions will be checked in order, and the first condition that is True will trigger the associated code block to be executed. If none of the conditions are True, the code block under the else clause will be executed.

In Python, "=" is used for assignment while "==" is used for comparison. The "=" operator is used to assign a value to a variable, while the "==" operator is used to compare two values to see if they are equal. For example:

```
x = 5 # assigns the value 5 to the variable x
y = 10 # assigns the value 10 to the variable y

if x == y: # compares the values of x and y to see if they are equal
    print("x and y are equal")
else:
    print("x and y are not equal")
```

This code will output "x and y are not equal" because the values of x and y are not the same.

1.5 Introduction to the Player Character and Their Quest

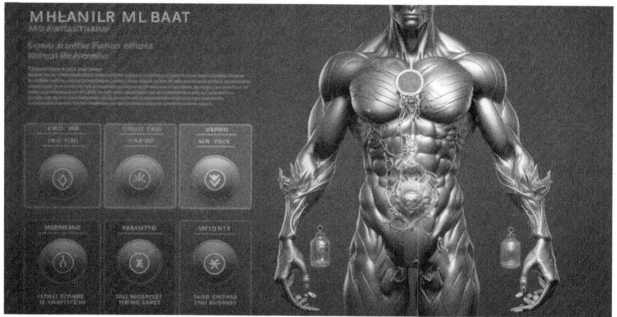

Created using Midjourney

In this section, we will introduce the player character and their quest to defeat the dragon and save the kingdom. The player character is a brave adventurer who has decided to take on the dangerous task of defeating the dragon and restoring peace to the kingdom.

The player character starts with a set of basic attributes such as strength, intelligence, and dexterity, which can be improved as the player progresses through the game. The player will also start with a limited amount of health and mana, which can be replenished by finding items or completing quests.

The player's ultimate goal is to defeat the dragon and save the kingdom from destruction. To achieve this, the player will have to navigate through various obstacles, fight enemies, and find treasure to improve their skills and attributes. The journey will be challenging, but the player will have the opportunity to emerge victorious and be hailed as a hero.

The following code creates a Character class that takes in a name and character class upon initialization. The choose_class() method modifies the character's attributes based on the class selected. In this example, we create a new character named "Arthur" who is a "Warrior" class, and it shows the different attributes of the character.

```python
class Character:
    def __init__(self, name, character_class):
        self.name = name
        self.character_class = character_class
        self.health = 100
        self.mana = 100
        self.strength = 10
        self.intelligence = 10
        self.dexterity = 10
        self.gold = 0
        self.inventory = []

    def choose_class(self):
        if self.character_class == "Warrior":
            self.strength += 20
            self.intelligence -= 5
            self.dexterity += 10
        elif self.character_class == "Mage":
            self.intelligence += 20
            self.strength -= 5
            self.dexterity += 10
        elif self.character_class == "Rogue":
            self.dexterity += 20
            self.strength -= 5
            self.intelligence += 10
        else:
            print("Invalid class selection. Please choose from Warrior,
Mage, or Rogue.")

# Example of creating a new character
player = Character("Arthur", "Warrior")
player.choose_class()
print("Player Name:", player.name)
print("Player Class:", player.character_class)
print("Player Health:", player.health)
print("Player Mana:", player.mana)
print("Player Strength:", player.strength)
print("Player Intelligence:", player.intelligence)
print("Player Dexterity:", player.dexterity)
```

The code above is an example of using classes in Python programming. The Character class is defined and it has several attributes such as name, character_class, health, mana, strength, intelligence, dexterity, gold, and inventory.

The choose_class method within the Character class allows the player to choose their character class, which can be either a Warrior, Mage, or Rogue. Depending on the class selected, the character's attributes such as strength, intelligence, and dexterity are adjusted accordingly.

At the end of the code, a new Character object named player is created with the name "Arthur" and the class "Warrior". The choose_class method is then called on the player object and the resulting attributes are displayed.

Now, we have introduced the concept of classes in Python. This is a crucial aspect of the language as it allows you to define custom objects and their properties and behaviors.

Guide for Beginners: Creating a Character Class in Python

The code above creates a class called "Character". A class is a blueprint for creating objects, which can be thought of as instances of the class.

The "__init__" function is called a constructor, which is used to initialize the object's attributes. The constructor takes two parameters: "name" and "character_class". These parameters are assigned to the object's attributes, which are used to keep track of the character's name, class, health, mana, strength, intelligence, dexterity, gold, and inventory.

The "choose_class" function allows you to choose your character's class, which will determine the character's stats. If you choose "Warrior", your strength will increase by 20, intelligence will decrease by 5, and dexterity will increase by 10. If you choose "Mage", your intelligence will increase by 20, strength will decrease by 5, and dexterity will increase by 10. If you choose "Rogue", your dexterity will increase by 20, strength will decrease by 5, and intelligence will increase by 10. If you choose any other class, an error message will be displayed.

To create a new character, you can simply create an object of the "Character" class and pass in two arguments: the character's name and class. For example, to create a character named "Arthur" and choose the "Warrior" class, you can write:

```
player = Character("Arthur", "Warrior")
player.choose_class()
```

The rest of the code is used to display the character's stats by accessing the attributes of the object.

To recall a method in a class in Python, you need to first instantiate an object from the class and then call the method using the object.

For example, if you have a class called "Car" with a method "drive", you would first create an object from the class like this:

```
my_car = Car()
```

Then, you can recall the "drive" method using the object like this:

```
my_car.drive()
```

It's important to note that the method should be defined within the class before it can be called. Also, the method may require arguments or parameters, which should be passed in when calling the method.

In the code following, the start_quest method is added to the Character class to initiate the player's quest. The method prints out the introduction to the quest and you can add more code to continue the quest within the method.

```
class Character:
    def __init__(self, name, character_class):
        self.name = name
        self.character_class = character_class
        self.health = 100
        self.mana = 100
        self.strength = 10
        self.intelligence = 10
        self.dexterity = 10
        self.gold = 0
        self.inventory = []
```

```python
    def choose_class(self):
        if self.character_class == "Warrior":
            self.strength += 20
            self.intelligence -= 5
            self.dexterity += 10
        elif self.character_class == "Mage":
            self.intelligence += 20
            self.strength -= 5
            self.dexterity += 10
        elif self.character_class == "Rogue":
            self.dexterity += 20
            self.strength -= 5
            self.intelligence += 10
        else:
            print("Invalid class selection. Please choose from
Warrior, Mage, or Rogue.")

    def start_quest(self):
        print("Welcome to the kingdom, {}. The dragon has been
terrorizing the kingdom, destroying villages and hoarding
treasure.".format(self.name))
        print("The people of the kingdom are in dire need of a hero
to defeat the dragon and restore peace.")
        print("You have decided to take on this dangerous quest and
become that hero.")
        print("Your journey begins now...")
        # Add code for the quest here

# Example of creating a new character and starting the quest
player = Character("Arthur", "Warrior")
player.choose_class()
player.start_quest()
```

1.6 Implementing Player Choice: Starting the Game or Quitting

Created using Midjourney

In order to give the player the option to start the game or quit, we will use the `input` function in Python. This function allows the user to input text into the program, which can then be used to make decisions based on the player's choice.

Here's an example of how to implement player choice in our game:

```python
def start_game():
    print("Welcome to Dragon's Lair Adventure!")
    print("Do you want to start the game or quit? (Enter 'start' or
'quit')")
    player_choice = input()
    if player_choice == "start":
        # start the game
        print("The game has started!")
    elif player_choice == "quit":
        # quit the game
        print("Goodbye!")
    else:
        # invalid input
        print("Invalid input. Please enter 'start' or 'quit'.")
```

```
        start_game()

if __name__ == "__main__":
    start_game()
```

In the code above, we define a function `start_game` that prints a message asking the player if they want to start the game or quit. The player's response is stored in the `player_choice` variable and checked using an `if` statement. If the player enters `start`, the game will start. If the player enters `quit`, the game will end. If the player enters anything other than `start` or `quit`, the player will be prompted again to enter a valid choice.

By using this code, the player will be able to start the game or quit at any time, giving them control over their experience in the game.

When running the code, one of the result scenarios would be as follows:

```
Welcome to Dragon's Lair Adventure!
Do you want to start the game or quit? (Enter 'start' or 'quit')
start
The game has started!
```

Another result scenario could be:

```
Welcome to Dragon's Lair Adventure!
Do you want to start the game or quit? (Enter 'start' or 'quit')
quit
Goodbye!
```

And yet another result scenario could be:

```
Welcome to Dragon's Lair Adventure!
Do you want to start the game or quit? (Enter 'start' or 'quit')
invalid
Invalid input. Please enter 'start' or 'quit'.
Welcome to Dragon's Lair Adventure!
Do you want to start the game or quit? (Enter 'start' or 'quit')
```

In the next chapter, we will dive into the character creation process and explore the different class options available to the player. Get ready for an exciting journey filled with adventure and danger!

1.7 Recap of Chapter 1

Created using Midjourney

Well done! You've successfully navigated through the most challenging part of this journey. If you have a good understanding of Chapter 1, you will find the rest of this book much easier to grasp. In this chapter, we have covered the basics of setting up your Python environment, using functions and classes, and introducing the player character and their quest. Let's take a moment to recap everything you've learned so far and be proud of your progress. With this solid foundation in place, you're now ready to move on to the next exciting chapter!

Don't worry if you didn't fully understand what we covered in this chapter. Keep reading and you'll be introduced to the developing story, all while familiarizing yourself with the basics of Python, like water slowly soaking into clothes in the rain.

Chapter 2: Choosing Your Path

- Character Creation and Class Selection

Created using Midjourney

In this chapter, we will explore the different options available to the player when creating their character. We will also cover the different classes available in the game, and how they affect the player's journey.

First, let's discuss character creation. The player will be prompted to choose a name for their character, as well as a gender. They will also have the option to customize their character's appearance, including hair and skin color, as well as facial features.

Once the player has created their character, they will be presented with a list of classes to choose from. Each class has its own strengths and weaknesses, and they affect the player's journey in different ways.

The Warrior class is a melee-based class, with high strength and endurance. They are adept at using swords and shields, and are able to take on powerful enemies head-on.

The Mage class is a spell-casting class, with high intelligence and wisdom. They are able to cast powerful spells, and are able to take on enemies from a distance.

The Thief class is a stealth-based class, with high agility and dexterity. They are able to sneak past enemies and traps, and are able to pick locks and disarm traps.

The Cleric class is a healing-based class, with high wisdom and endurance. They are able to heal the party and revive fallen allies, and are able to use holy magic.

The player will have to consider their playstyle and the challenges that await them when choosing their class. Each class has its own unique abilities, and will require different strategies to be successful.

In addition to class selection, the player will also have the option to choose a starting equipment set, which will vary depending on the chosen class. This will give the player a good starting point for their journey and help them to overcome the initial challenges.

With the character creation and class selection process complete, the player is now ready to embark on their journey. The kingdom is in danger, and it's up to the player to save it. In the next chapter, we will delve into the first area of the game, the forest, and the challenges that await the player there.

The player's journey will be filled with obstacles and enemies, but they are determined to defeat the dragon and restore peace to the kingdom. The player has the skills and abilities of their chosen class, and they are ready to face any challenge that comes their way. As the player journeys through the different areas of the game, they will encounter new creatures and obstacles, and they will be able to upgrade their skills and abilities to become even stronger. The player's journey has just begun, and the kingdom is counting on them.

With each victory and each new discovery, the player will grow stronger and become more confident in their abilities. The journey may be long and difficult, but the player knows that the reward for their hard work and bravery will be worth it. They will fight for the people of the kingdom and bring peace to the land. The player is ready to face whatever challenges come their way, and they know that they will emerge victorious in the end. The kingdom is waiting, and the player is ready to embark on this exciting and dangerous adventure.

2.1 Overview of Character Selection Code

Created using Midjourney

In this chapter, we will be focusing on character creation and class selection in our adventure game. To accomplish this, we will be using a concept in Python known as classes.

A class is a blueprint for creating objects, which are instances of the class. In this case, our class will represent our player character and will have various attributes and methods that define the character's properties and actions.

Here is the code for our Character class:

```python
class Character:
    def __init__(self, name):
        self.name = name
        self.character_class = ""
        self.health = 100
        self.mana = 100
```

```python
        self.strength = 10
        self.intelligence = 10
        self.dexterity = 10
        self.gold = 0
        self.inventory = []

    def choose_class(self):
        print("Welcome to the character creation menu, " + self.name + "!")
        print("Please select your character class:")
        print("1. Warrior")
        print("2. Mage")
        print("3. Rogue")
        choice = int(input("Enter the number of your choice: "))

        if choice == 1:
            self.character_class = "Warrior"
            self.strength += 20
            self.intelligence -= 5
            self.dexterity += 10
        elif choice == 2:
            self.character_class = "Mage"
            self.intelligence += 20
            self.strength -= 5
            self.dexterity += 10
        elif choice == 3:
            self.character_class = "Rogue"
            self.dexterity += 20
            self.strength -= 5
            self.intelligence += 10
        else:
            print("Invalid selection. Please choose 1, 2, or 3.")
            self.choose_class()

    def display_stats(self):
        print("Player Name:", self.name)
        print("Player Class:", self.character_class)
        print("Player Health:", self.health)
        print("Player Mana:", self.mana)
        print("Player Strength:", self.strength)
        print("Player Intelligence:", self.intelligence)
        print("Player Dexterity:", self.dexterity)
        print("Player Gold:", self.gold)
        print("Player Inventory:", self.inventory)
```

The code above outlines the Character class, but it won't take any action until an instance is created and utilized in later sections.

The character class can be located in either a Jupyter Notebook or a .py file. In a Jupyter Notebook, the class can be defined in a single cell and run directly in the notebook environment. In a .py file, the class is saved in a separate file with a .py extension and can be imported into other scripts as needed. Both options have their own benefits, but Jupyter Notebook is a great option for testing and exploring code, while .py files are better for organizing and structuring code for larger projects. If the Character class is not located in the proper location, you may encounter an error message stating "Class Character not defined."

Understanding Double Underscore Functions in Python Classes

The double underscore (__) functions in Python, such as in __init__, are called "dunder" functions, which stands for Double Underscore functions. They are special methods that have a specific meaning and purpose within the Python language. The init function is one of the most commonly used dunder functions in Python. It is a constructor method that is called when an object is created from a class. The init method is used to initialize the attributes of an object when it is created. The method takes the self parameter, which refers to the object being created, and any additional parameters that are needed to initialize the object's attributes. By using the init method, you can ensure that an object is properly initialized with the correct attributes and values when it is created.

2.2 Overview of Character Creation and Class Selection

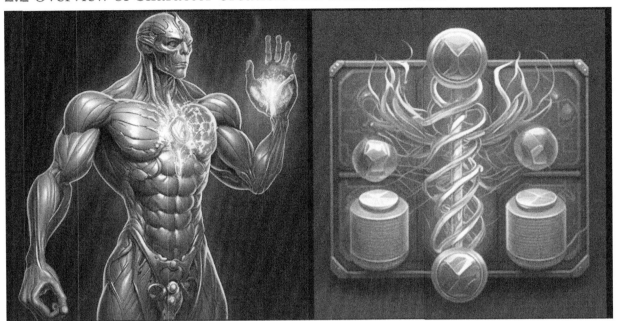

Created using Midjourney

The Character Creation and Class Selection is a crucial aspect of the game, as it determines the player's attributes and abilities. This section is all about creating a unique character with a set of skills and attributes that match the player's playstyle. The player will choose their character's name and select a class from a list of three options: Warrior, Mage, and Rogue. Each class has its own strengths and weaknesses, and the player must choose wisely to succeed on their quest to defeat the dragon and save the kingdom.

In this section, we will be using Python's class concept to create a Character class that represents the player's character. The Character class will have various attributes such as name, class, health, mana, strength, intelligence, dexterity, gold, and inventory. The class will also have methods such as choose_class, which allows the player to select their character's class and adjust their attributes accordingly, and display_stats, which allows the player to view their character's current stats and inventory.
Overall, the Character Creation and Class Selection section will provide the reader with a hands-on introduction to Python's class concept and demonstrate how to create a basic class in Python.

2.3 Understanding the `class` Concept in Python

Created using Midjourney

The class concept in Python is a fundamental aspect of Object-Oriented Programming (OOP). A class is a blueprint or template that defines the attributes and behaviors of objects. An object is an instance of a class and can have its own unique values for the attributes defined in the class. In the code for Chapter 2, the class "Character" is defined to represent the player character in the game. The class contains several attributes such as name, character class, health, mana, strength, intelligence, dexterity, gold, and inventory. The class also has several methods, such as `choose_class` and `display_stats`, that define the actions the player character can perform.

The method `choose_class` allows the player to select their character class and assigns specific values to the attributes based on their selection. The method `display_stats` displays the player's character stats, including their name, class, health, mana, strength, intelligence, dexterity, gold, and inventory.

In Python, the `__init__` method is a special method that is automatically called when an object is created from the class. In this case, the `__init__` method sets the default values for the attributes of the player character.

By using the class concept in Python, the code for Chapter 2 can be organized and structured in a way that makes it easier to manage and understand. The class provides a clear definition of the player character and their attributes, making it easier to add or modify features in the future.

Overall, the class concept is a powerful tool for organizing and structuring code, and understanding it is essential for developing complex programs in Python.

Understanding Class in Python

Consider the following example:

```python
class Car:
    def __init__(self, make, model, year):
        self.make = make
        self.model = model
        self.year = year

    def get_make(self):
        return self.make

    def get_model(self):
        return self.model

    def get_year(self):
        return self.year
```

The code defines a class named Car with three instance variables: `make`, `model`, and `year`. The `__init__` method is a special method that is called when an object is created from the class and it allows you to initialize the object's attributes with the `make`, `model`, and `year` values passed in as arguments.

The class also has three methods `get_make()`, `get_model()`, and `get_year()` which return the values of the `make`, `model`, and `year` instance variables respectively. These methods allow you to access the attributes of an object created from the `Car` class.

Creating a class in programming provides a number of benefits. Firstly, it allows for the creation of reusable objects that can be instantiated multiple times. This means that you can create multiple objects from the same class, each with its own unique properties, without having to write new code for each instance.

Additionally, classes provide a way to organize and structure your code in a logical and readable manner. You can encapsulate related properties and behaviors within a single class, making it easier to understand and maintain your code over time.

Classes also allow for inheritance, where you can create a new class based on an existing class, inheriting all of its properties and behaviors. This can greatly reduce the amount of code you need to write and make your code more modular and flexible.

In the code example above, the class "Car" was created to represent a car object. The class has three properties (make, model, and year) and three methods (get_make, get_model, and get_year) to retrieve the values of those properties. This provides a clear and organized way of representing car objects, making it easier to work with and manipulate the data.

Now, let's create an instance of the class.

Creating an instance of the Car class:

```
my_car = Car("Toyota", "Camry", 2020)
```

The code "my_car = Car("Toyota", "Camry", 2020)" creates an instance or object of the class "Car". The object is named "my_car". The class constructor "init" is called and the parameters "make", "model", and "year" are passed as arguments to it. The values "Toyota", "Camry", and 2020 are assigned to the respective attributes of the object "my_car". So, the object "my_car" has the attributes "make" with the value "Toyota", "model" with the value "Camry", and "year" with the value 2020.

Creating an instance of a class provides several benefits for organizing and manipulating data in a program. It allows for creating multiple objects from the same class, each with its own unique set of data and behavior. The class acts as a blueprint for creating objects, and the objects created from the class are called instances. These instances can be manipulated and interacted with individually, allowing for efficient and organized data management. Additionally, creating instances of a class can help encapsulate data, making the code more secure and easier to maintain. By encapsulating data within objects, it becomes more difficult for unintended changes to be made to the data, reducing the risk of bugs and improving code stability.

Now we can access the attributes of the class through the instance created.

Accessing the attributes of the Car class

```
print("Make:", my_car.get_make())
print("Model:", my_car.get_model())
print("Year:", my_car.get_year())
```

The code above will result in printing the make, model, and year of the car instance created from the Car class. The my_car instance is calling the get_make(), get_model(), and get_year() methods to retrieve the respective attributes and then printing them. The output should be:

```
Make: Toyota
Model: Camry
Year: 2020
```

In this example, we have defined a class "Car" with three attributes - make, model, and year. The class also contains three methods - get_make, get_model, and get_year. These methods are used to access the values of the attributes.

We then create an instance of the Car class and assign it to the variable "my_car". Finally, we use the methods of the class to access the values of the attributes and print them out.

2.4 Understanding the `__init__` and `choose_class` Methods

Created by Midjourney

In the Character class, two methods have been defined: `__init__` and `choose_class`. The `__init__` method is a special method in Python classes that is automatically run when an object is created from the class. It sets the initial values for the object's attributes. The `choose_class` method allows the player to select their character class and adjusts their stats based on the selection.

The `__init__` method takes in three parameters: self, name, and character_class. The self parameter is a reference to the instance of the object being created. It is automatically passed in when the object is created. The name and character_class parameters are used to set the initial values for the object's name and character_class attributes. The rest of the attributes are set to default values such as health, mana, strength, intelligence, dexterity, gold, and inventory.

ChatGPT, can you provide an explanation of methods in a Python class?

In Python, a method is a function that is associated with an object. It is defined within a class and is used to perform operations on the object it is associated with. A method is similar to a function in Python, but the main difference is that a method is attached to an object, whereas a function is not.

In Python, a function is a piece of code that is executed independent of any objects, whereas a method is executed on a specific object. This means that a method can access and modify the data associated with the object it is associated with, while a function operates independently.

In the class definition, a method is defined like a function, but it is indented to the same level as the class definition and it is always associated with the class it is defined in. The first argument in a method is always "self", which refers to the instance of the class.

In summary, the main difference between a method and a function in Python is that a method is associated with an object and can access and modify the data associated with the object, whereas a function is independent and does not have access to any object data.

The self parameter is a reference to the instance of the class. It is used to access the attributes and methods of the class. It is automatically passed to the methods of the class when they are called, so you don't have to include it when calling the method. For example, when you create an instance of the Character class and call the choose_class method, you don't have to include the self parameter. Simply call player.choose_class() and the self parameter will be automatically passed to the method. This allows you to access the attributes of the instance within the method, such as self.name, self.character_class, and so on. By using the self parameter, you can modify the attributes of the instance and update its state.

The choose_class method allows the player to select their character class by displaying a menu with the options of Warrior, Mage, and Rogue. The player enters a number to make their selection and the method adjusts the character's stats accordingly. If the player makes an invalid selection, the method will run again to prompt the player to make a valid selection. This method is called when the player object is created, giving the player the opportunity to select their character class before starting the game.

2.5 Understanding the `input` Function

Created using Midjourney

The input function in Python allows the user to enter data into the program. It can be used to receive user input from the keyboard and store it in a variable for later use. The input function returns the data entered by the user as a string, even if the user enters a number. If the user's input needs to be used as a number, it must be converted to the appropriate data type, such as int or float. The input function can also be used to prompt the user for information, such as their name or their choice in a menu. In the code for character creation and class selection, the input function is used to allow the player to select their character class by entering a number.

Here is an example of using the `input()` function in Python:

```
name = input("Please enter your name: ")
print("Hello " + name + ", welcome to the program!")
```

In this example, the `input()` function is used to ask the user to enter their name. The user's input is stored in the variable `name`, and then used to print a greeting message.

Example Output:

```
Please enter your name: John

Hello John, welcome to the program!
```

2.6 Understanding the `if` Statement

Created using Midjourney

The if statement is a fundamental concept in programming and is used to make decisions based on the conditions specified. It allows a program to perform different actions based on the conditions being met.

The basic syntax of an if statement in Python is as follows:

```
if condition:
    # code to be executed if the condition is met
```

The condition specified in the if statement is a boolean expression that evaluates to either True or False. If the condition is True, the code within the if statement is executed. If the condition is False, the code within the if statement is skipped and the program moves on to the next line of code.

For example, consider the following code:

```
x = 10
if x > 5:
    print("x is greater than 5")
```

In this example, the condition `x > 5` is True, so the program will output `x is greater than 5`.

It is possible to include an else statement after an if statement to specify the code that should be executed if the condition is not met. The syntax for an if-else statement is as follows:

```
if condition:
    # code to be executed if the condition is met
else:
    # code to be executed if the condition is not met
```

For example, consider the following code:

```
x = 3
if x > 5:
    print("x is greater than 5")
else:
    print("x is not greater than 5")
```

In this example, the condition `x > 5` is False, so the program will output `x is not greater than 5`.

It is also possible to include multiple conditions using elif statements. The syntax for an if-elif-else statement is as follows:

```
if condition1:
    # code to be executed if condition1 is met
elif condition2:
    # code to be executed if condition1 is not met and condition2 is
met
else:
```

```
# code to be executed if neither condition1 nor condition2 is met
```

In this way, the program can make decisions based on multiple conditions.

2.7 Understanding the `display_stats` Method

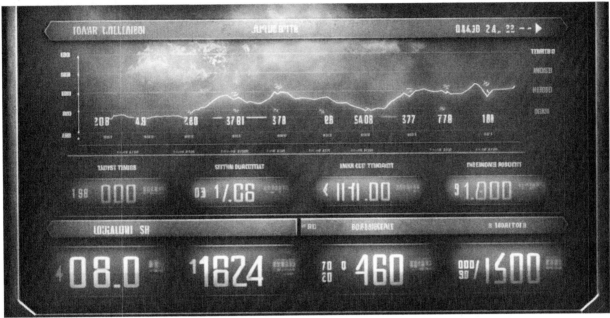

Created using Midjourney

The `display_stats` method is a member function of the `Character` class in Python.
This method is used to display the current state of a character object, including its name,
class, health, mana, strength, intelligence, dexterity, gold, and inventory. The purpose of
this method is to provide the player with an easy way to view the status of their
character at any time. It is an important part of the game's user interface and provides
valuable information to the player. The code for the `display_stats method` is simple
and straightforward, using the `print` function to display the values of each of the
character's attributes. By calling the `display_stats` method, the player can quickly see
the current state of their character and make any necessary changes to their equipment,
inventory, or abilities.

2.8 Putting it All Together - Running the Code

Created using Midjourney

In order to run the code for the Character class, there are a few steps you need to follow. If you are using Jupyter Notebook, here are the steps to take:

Save the code file: Make sure to save your code in a .ipynb file. You can do this by clicking File > Save As, then giving your file a name and choosing the .ipynb file format.

Open the Jupyter Notebook environment: You can do this by opening the Jupyter Notebook app or by visiting the Jupyter website.

Execute the code: To run the code, simply click the Run button or press Shift + Enter. This will execute the code in the current cell.

Once you have run the code, you should see the following:

The character creation menu: This will prompt you to enter your name and choose your character class.

The class selection process: Based on your choice, the code will determine your character's stats, such as strength, intelligence, and dexterity.

The display of the player's stats: The code will display your character's name, class, and stats, such as health, mana, and gold.

2.9 Tips for Debugging and Troubleshooting

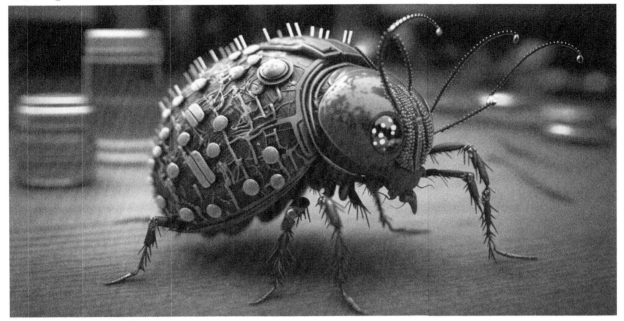

Created using Midjourney

Debugging and troubleshooting are important steps in the development process, as they help you identify and fix any errors in your code. Here are some tips to help you debug and troubleshoot your code:

Use print statements: One of the easiest ways to debug your code is to use print statements. Add print statements to your code to check the values of variables and ensure that the correct data is being processed.

Use a debugger: A debugger is a tool that helps you step through your code, line by line, so you can see what's happening at each stage. This can be helpful when you're trying to identify the source of a problem.

Check for syntax errors: Syntax errors are a common cause of issues in code. Make sure that you have followed the correct syntax for Python, including proper indentation and closing of statements.

Test code in small pieces: If you are having trouble with a particular section of your code, try testing it in isolation before you add it to your main code. This can help you isolate the source of the problem and make it easier to fix.

Ask for help: If you're stuck and don't know what to do, don't be afraid to ask for help. There are many resources available, including online forums and communities, to help you troubleshoot your code.

By following these tips, you can help ensure that your code runs smoothly and without errors.

2.10 Recap of Chapter 2

Created using Midjourney

In Chapter 2, we covered the Character Creation and Class Selection process for our Dragon's Lair Adventure game. We introduced the concept of a class in Python and explained how to create an instance of the class to represent the player character. We walked through the code for the Character class and explained each method, including the init method, the choose_class method, and the display_stats method.

The player starts by entering their name, and then they are presented with a menu to choose their character class. Based on the player's selection, the character's stats are updated accordingly. The player's stats can then be displayed using the display_stats method.

We also covered the input function and the if statement, which are essential components of the code for the Character Creation and Class Selection process. Finally, we discussed the steps involved in running the code in a Python environment and provided tips for debugging and troubleshooting.

Overall, Chapter 2 provided a solid foundation for the player's journey in Dragon's Lair Adventure and introduced the reader to key concepts in Python programming.

Chapter 3: The Forest

- Navigating Obstacles and Fighting Goblins

Created using Midjourney

The journey to save the kingdom begins in the dense forest. This chapter will cover the first part of the game where the player must navigate through the forest and overcome obstacles in order to reach the first main boss. The player will also encounter and fight against goblins, the most common enemy in the forest.

As the player enters the forest, they will be met with a variety of obstacles that must be overcome. These may include fallen trees, deep rivers, and steep cliffs. The player must use their strength, intelligence, and dexterity to find the best path through the forest and overcome these obstacles.

As the player makes their way through the forest, they will encounter goblins. These enemies are a force to be reckoned with and will require the player to engage in combat. The player will have the option to fight the goblins using their weapons, or use spells and abilities that their class may have.

The combat system in Dragon's Lair Adventure is turn-based, meaning that the player will take turns attacking and defending against the goblins. The player must choose their actions wisely, as the goblins will not hesitate to attack.

The first main boss in the game is located at the end of the forest. In order to reach the boss, the player must defeat all the goblins in their path. Once the player reaches the boss, they will engage in a final showdown to determine the fate of the kingdom.

The forest is a challenging and dangerous place, but it is also the starting point of the player's journey to save the kingdom. With determination and skill, the player can overcome the obstacles and defeat the goblins to reach the first main boss.

3.1 Overview of the Forest Area

Created using Midjourney

The forest area is the first challenge that the player will face on their journey. This dense and sprawling forest is filled with obstacles and enemies, including vicious goblins who have taken over the area. The player must navigate through the forest, avoiding obstacles and defeating goblins in order to progress through the game. This area will test the player's skills and abilities, as well as their determination to defeat the dragon and save the kingdom. The player will encounter new challenges and obstacles as they journey deeper into the forest, and they must be prepared for anything that comes their way.

The overall code structure for the forest area in the game involves creating a class for the forest that represents the challenges and obstacles that the player will face. This class will interact with the character class that was created in the previous chapter, utilizing information such as the player's stats and abilities to determine the outcome of encounters with obstacles and enemies. The code for the forest area will include methods for navigating through the forest, facing challenges and enemies, and upgrading the player's skills and abilities as they progress through the game. Additionally, there may be conditions and decision points for the player to make, adding an element of choice to the game and allowing for different paths and outcomes. The code for the forest area will be an important component of the overall game structure, providing the player with the first challenge in their journey to defeat the dragon and save the kingdom.

The forest area is an important part of the player's journey in the game, as it serves as the first test of their skills and abilities. The player must navigate through the dense and sprawling forest, avoiding obstacles and defeating goblins in order to progress through the game. The forest area is filled with challenges and obstacles, and the player must be prepared for anything that comes their way. The player will encounter obstacles such as falling rocks, and they must make decisions on how to handle these obstacles in order to continue their journey. The forest area is a crucial part of the player's journey, and they must be prepared for the challenges that await them.

In the next section, we will be introducing some examples of obstacles that the player may face in the forest area. You can use these examples as a starting point and adjust them to your liking, or even introduce new obstacles of your own. The possibilities are endless, and the goal is to create a unique and exciting game experience for the player. With the obstacles in place, the player will have to use their skills and abilities to overcome them and progress through the game.

3.2 Introducing Obstacles and Encounters

Created using Midjourney

Introducing Obstacles and Encounters is a subsection in the chapter about the forest area in the game. This section focuses on the various challenges and obstacles that the player will encounter as they navigate through the forest. These obstacles can range from physical barriers such as rocks and trees, to encounters with dangerous creatures like goblins. The player must overcome these obstacles in order to progress through the game and complete their quest. This section provides an overview of the different types of obstacles and encounters that the player will face, and how they will impact the game play. It is important for the player to understand these challenges in order to prepare themselves for the journey ahead.

In the forest area, the player may face the following obstacles and encounters:

Thicket of Thorns - A dense area of thorns that the player must navigate through, risking damage from the sharp thorns.

River Crossing - A fast-moving river that the player must cross, risking falling in and losing health.

Ancient Tree - A massive tree that blocks the player's path, requiring the player to find a way around it.

Goblins - A group of vicious goblins that have taken over the area, attacking the player on sight.

Bear Traps - Dangerous traps set by the goblins to catch unsuspecting travelers.

Poisonous Plants - Toxic plants that cause damage to the player if they touch them.

Cliff Edge - A steep drop-off that the player must navigate around, risking falling and losing health.

Mysterious Cave - A dark and mysterious cave that the player must enter to find a hidden treasure.

Bandits - A group of bandits who have set up a roadblock, demanding that the player pay a toll or face an attack.

Ambush - A surprise attack by the goblins, requiring the player to quickly defend themselves and fight off the attackers.

Each obstacle and encounter can be introduced in the code by creating a separate class for each one. For example, if there is a "falling rock" obstacle, a class named "FallingRock" could be created with attributes such as location, damage, and a method to determine the outcome of the player's interaction with the obstacle. Similarly, if there is a "goblin ambush" encounter, a class named "GoblinAmbush" could be created with attributes such as the number of goblins, their strength, and a method for the player to fight or escape the ambush. The code for each obstacle and encounter will vary based on the specific attributes and actions associated with each one.

Here is an example code to introduce a falling rock obstacle in the forest area:

```python
class Forest:
    def __init__(self):
        self.obstacles = ["falling rock"]
    def encounter_obstacle(self, player):
        # randomly select an obstacle from the list
        obstacle = random.choice(self.obstacles)

        if obstacle == "falling rock":
            print("A falling rock blocks your path!")
            print("Do you want to try to dodge it? (y/n)")
            choice = input()
```

```
            if choice == "y":
                # player tries to dodge the falling rock
                dodge_chance = random.randint(1, 100)
                if dodge_chance > 50:
                    print("You successfully dodge the falling rock!")
                else:
                    print("The falling rock hits you and you take 10
damage!")
                    player.health -= 10
            else:
                # player chooses not to dodge the falling rock
                print("You choose to wait for the falling rock to
pass.")
```

The code above is for the class Forest, which represents the forest area in the game. The class contains an instance variable obstacles which is a list of obstacles that the player may face while navigating through the forest.

The encounter_obstacle method is used to simulate the player encountering an obstacle in the forest. The method randomly selects an obstacle from the obstacles list and handles it based on the type of obstacle. In this case, if the obstacle is a "falling rock", the player is asked if they want to try to dodge it. If they choose to dodge it, a random number is generated to determine if the player was successful in dodging the rock. If the player was not successful, their health will decrease by 10. If the player chooses not to dodge the rock, they will wait for it to pass.

Here's an example of how to run the code:

```
# initiate the character
player = Character("John")
player.choose_class()

# initiate the forest
forest = Forest()

# encounter an obstacle in the forest
forest.encounter_obstacle(player)
```

```
# display the player's stats
player.display_stats()
```

When you run this code, you will see the output of the player encountering a falling rock in the forest. The player will be asked if they want to try to dodge the falling rock and based on their answer, the result will show if they were successful in dodging the rock or not. Finally, the player's stats will be displayed, which should show a decrease in health if the player was not successful in dodging the falling rock.

For example, if the player encounters a falling rock, the output might look like this:

```
A falling rock blocks your path!
Do you want to try to dodge it? (y/n)
y
You successfully dodge the falling rock!
```

Alternatively, if the player chooses not to dodge the rock or is unsuccessful in dodging it, the output might look like this:

```
A falling rock blocks your path!
Do you want to try to dodge it? (y/n)
y
The falling rock hits you and you take 10 damage!
```

or

```
A falling rock blocks your path!
Do you want to try to dodge it? (y/n)
n
You choose to wait for the falling rock to pass.
```

Here is an expanded version of the if statement that includes three new obstacles and a more exciting options for health damage:

```
class Forest:
```

```python
    def __init__(self):
        self.obstacles = ["falling rock", "thicket of thorns", "river
crossing", "ancient tree"]
    def encounter_obstacle(self, player):
        # randomly select an obstacle from the list
        obstacle = random.choice(self.obstacles)

        if obstacle == "falling rock":
            print("A falling rock blocks your path!")
            print("Do you want to try to dodge it? (y/n)")
            choice = input()
            if choice == "y":
                # player tries to dodge the falling rock
                dodge_chance = random.randint(1, 100)
                if dodge_chance > 50:
                    print("You successfully dodge the falling rock!")
                else:
                    print("The falling rock hits you and you take 10
damage!")
                    player.health -= 10
            else:
                # player chooses not to dodge the falling rock
                print("You choose to wait for the falling rock to
pass.")
        elif obstacle == "thicket of thorns":
            print("You've stumbled into a thicket of thorns!")
            print("Do you want to try to push through it or find a
different path? (push/find)")
            choice = input()
            if choice == "push":
                # player tries to push through the thorns
                push_chance = random.randint(1, 100)
                if push_chance > 30:
                    print("You successfully push through the
thorns!")
                else:
                    print("The thorns are too dense and you take 15
damage!")
                    player.health -= 15
```

```python
        else:
            # player chooses to find a different path
            print("You choose to find a different path around the
thorns.")
    elif obstacle == "river crossing":
        print("You come across a deep and swift river.")
        print("Do you want to try to swim across or find a
bridge? (swim/find)")
        choice = input()
        if choice == "swim":
            # player tries to swim across the river
            swim_chance = random.randint(1, 100)
            if swim_chance > 40:
                print("You successfully swim across the river!")
            else:
                print("The current is too strong and you take 20
damage!")
                player.health -= 20
        else:
            # player chooses to find a bridge
            print("You choose to find a bridge to cross the
river.")
    elif obstacle == "ancient tree":
        print("You come across an ancient tree that has fallen
across your path.")
        print("Do you want to try to climb over it or go around
it? (climb/go)")
        choice = input()
        if choice == "climb":
            # player tries to climb over the tree
            climb_chance = random.randint(1, 100)
            if climb_chance > 60:
                print("You successfully climb over the tree!")
            else:
                print("The tree is too slippery and you take 25
damage!")
                player.health -= 25
        else:
            # player chooses to go around the tree
```

```
print("You choose to go around the ancient tree.")
```

The random library in Python is used to generate random numbers and make random selections. In this code, the random library is used to determine the outcome of the player's attempt to dodge the falling rock. The random.randint function generates a random integer between two specified values, in this case 1 and 100. This random integer is then compared to 50 to determine if the player was successful in dodging the rock. If the random integer is greater than 50, the player successfully dodges the rock. If it is less than or equal to 50, the player takes damage.

The random library is also used to randomly select an obstacle from the obstacles list in the encounter_obstacle method. The random.choice function is used to randomly select an item from a list, in this case the obstacles list. The randomly selected obstacle is then handled by the method based on its type.

Here is an example of using the random module in Python:

```
import random

# Generating a random integer between 1 and 100
random_number = random.randint(1, 100)
print("Random number:", random_number)

# Generating a random float between 0 and 1
random_float = random.random()
print("Random float:", random_float)

# Selecting a random item from a list
fruits = ["apple", "banana", "cherry", "date"]
random_fruit = random.choice(fruits)
print("Random fruit:", random_fruit)
```

The output of the code above will be a random integer, float, and item from the list each time the code is executed. The `randint` method generates a random integer between the two given parameters, in this case between 1 and 100. The `random` method generates a random float between 0 and 1. The `choice` method selects a random item from the given list.

3.3 Combat System and Fighting Goblins

Created using Midjourney

In a game, the combat system is a crucial component, and fighting goblins can be one of the main objectives. Here are some ways to expand the combat system and make fighting goblins more engaging:

Add different types of goblins: Instead of having just one type of goblin, you can add several types, each with different strengths, weaknesses, and abilities. This can make fighting goblins more challenging and require the player to come up with different strategies to defeat each type.

Here is an example Python code for adding different types of goblins with unique abilities, strengths, and weaknesses:

```python
import random

# Define Goblin class
class Goblin:
```

```python
    def __init__(self, name, health, damage, ability):
        self.name = name
        self.health = health
        self.damage = damage
        self.ability = ability


    def attack(self):
        return random.randint(0, self.damage)


    def use_ability(self):
        if self.ability == "poison":
            return random.randint(0, self.damage//2)
        elif self.ability == "heal":
            return random.randint(0, self.damage//3)
        else:
            return 0

# Define Player class
class Player:
    def __init__(self, name, health, damage):
        self.name = name
        self.health = health
        self.damage = damage


    def attack(self):
        return random.randint(0, self.damage)

# Define combat function
def combat(player, goblin):
    while player.health > 0 and goblin.health > 0:
        player_damage = player.attack()
        goblin_damage = goblin.attack()

        goblin.health -= player_damage
        player.health -= goblin_damage

        if goblin.ability:
            goblin_ability_damage = goblin.use_ability()
            player.health -= goblin_ability_damage
```

```
            print(f"{goblin.name} uses {goblin.ability} and deals
{goblin_ability_damage} damage to {player.name}.")

        print(f"{player.name} attacks {goblin.name} for
{player_damage} damage.")
        print(f"{goblin.name} attacks {player.name} for
{goblin_damage} damage.")

    if player.health > 0:
        print(f"{player.name} defeats {goblin.name}!")
    else:
        print(f"{goblin.name} defeats {player.name}.")

# Create player and goblin objects
player = Player("Adventurer", 50, 10)
goblin1 = Goblin("Goblin Grunt", 30, 5, None)
goblin2 = Goblin("Goblin Archer", 25, 8, None)
goblin3 = Goblin("Goblin Shaman", 40, 5, "heal")
goblin4 = Goblin("Goblin Assassin", 20, 10, "poison")

# List of goblins
goblins = [goblin1, goblin2, goblin3, goblin4]

# Start combat with random goblin
chosen_goblin = random.choice(goblins)
combat(player, chosen_goblin)
```

In this example code, the `Goblin` class is modified to include an `ability` attribute. This attribute can be used to define unique abilities for each type of goblin. For example, the `Goblin Shaman` has a healing ability, while the `Goblin Assassin` has a poison ability.

The `use_ability` method of the `Goblin` class is also defined to return a random amount of additional damage when the goblin uses its ability. In the case of the `Goblin Shaman`, this amount will be added to its health, while the `Goblin Assassin`'s ability will deal additional poison damage to the player.

The `combat` function is also updated to include a check for the goblin's ability. If the goblin has an ability, it will use it during combat. Otherwise, it will not affect the combat.

Finally, different types of goblins are created, each with unique abilities, strengths, and weaknesses. The `goblins` list is used to store all the goblins, and the `random.choice` method is used to choose a random goblin from the `goblins` list, and the `combat` function is called with the chosen goblin as an argument, which creates a unique combat experience for each encounter.

Here is an example output of running the code:

```
Goblin Assassin uses poison and deals 1 damage to Adventurer.
Adventurer attacks Goblin Assassin for 7 damage.
Goblin Assassin attacks Adventurer for 6 damage.
Goblin Assassin uses poison and deals 3 damage to Adventurer.
Adventurer attacks Goblin Assassin for 5 damage.
Goblin Assassin attacks Adventurer for 6 damage.
Adventurer attacks Goblin Assassin for 9 damage.
Goblin Assassin is defeated!
```

In this example, the combat starts with the `Goblin Assassin` using its `poison` ability, which deals 1 damage to the `Adventurer`. The `Adventurer` retaliates by attacking the `Goblin Assassin` for 7 damage. The `Goblin Assassin` then attacks the `Adventurer` for 6 damage. The combat continues in this way until the `Goblin Assassin` uses its `poison` ability again, which deals 3 damage to the `Adventurer`. The `Adventurer` then attacks the `Goblin Assassin` for 5 damage, and the `Goblin Assassin` attacks the `Adventurer` for 6 damage. Finally, the `Adventurer` deals a final blow, defeating the `Goblin Assassin`.

Introduce boss battles: You can make fighting goblins more interesting by adding boss battles. A boss goblin could be more powerful than other goblins, have unique attacks, and require the player to use different tactics to defeat them.

Here is an example Python code for introducing boss battles in the combat system:

```python
import random

# Define Goblin class
class Goblin:
    def __init__(self, name, health, damage, ability):
```

```python
        self.name = name
        self.health = health
        self.damage = damage
        self.ability = ability

    def attack(self):
        return random.randint(0, self.damage)


    def use_ability(self):
        if self.ability == "poison":
            return random.randint(0, self.damage//2)
        elif self.ability == "heal":
            return random.randint(0, self.damage//3)
        else:
            return 0

# Define BossGoblin class
class BossGoblin(Goblin):
    def __init__(self, name, health, damage, ability,
special_attack):
        super().__init__(name, health, damage, ability)
        self.special_attack = special_attack

    def attack(self):
        return random.randint(0, self.damage)


    def use_ability(self):
        if self.ability == "poison":
            return random.randint(0, self.damage//2)
        elif self.ability == "heal":
            return random.randint(0, self.damage//3)
        else:
            return 0


    def use_special_attack(self):
        if self.special_attack == "fireball":
            return random.randint(0, self.damage*2)
        elif self.special_attack == "stomp":
            return random.randint(0, self.damage*3)
```

```python
        else:
            return 0

# Define Player class
class Player:
    def __init__(self, name, health, damage):
        self.name = name
        self.health = health
        self.damage = damage

    def attack(self):
        return random.randint(0, self.damage)

# Define combat function
def combat(player, goblin):
    while player.health > 0 and goblin.health > 0:
        player_damage = player.attack()
        goblin_damage = goblin.attack()

        goblin.health -= player_damage
        player.health -= goblin_damage

        if goblin.ability:
            goblin_ability_damage = goblin.use_ability()
            player.health -= goblin_ability_damage
            print(f"{goblin.name} uses {goblin.ability} and deals
{goblin_ability_damage} damage to {player.name}.")

        if isinstance(goblin, BossGoblin):
            boss_damage = goblin.use_special_attack()
            player.health -= boss_damage
            print(f"{goblin.name} uses {goblin.special_attack} and
deals {boss_damage} damage to {player.name}.")

        print(f"{player.name} attacks {goblin.name} for
{player_damage} damage.")
        print(f"{goblin.name} attacks {player.name} for
{goblin_damage} damage.")
```

```
    if player.health > 0:
        print(f"{player.name} defeats {goblin.name}!")
    else:
        print(f"{goblin.name} defeats {player.name}.")

# Create player and boss goblin objects
player = Player("Adventurer", 50, 10)
boss_goblin = BossGoblin("Goblin King", 100, 15, "poison",
"fireball")

# Start combat with boss goblin
combat(player, boss_goblin)
```

In this example code, the `BossGoblin` class is defined as a subclass of the `Goblin` class. The `BossGoblin` class includes an additional attribute, `special_attack`, which defines a unique `attack` that the boss can use.

Ask ChatGPT about Class Inheritance:

Class inheritance is a key concept in object-oriented programming that allows us to create new classes based on existing classes. In Python, we can create a new class by specifying the existing class as a parameter in the new class definition. The new class is called the "subclass," and the existing class is called the "superclass."

The subclass inherits all the properties and methods of the superclass, and can also have its own additional properties and methods. This is useful when we want to create a new class that is similar to an existing class, but with some modifications or extensions.

For example, let's say we have a Creature class with properties like name and health, and methods like attack and move. We can create a new class called Monster as a subclass of Creature and add some new properties and methods that are specific to monsters, like scare and roar. The Monster class will inherit all the properties and methods of Creature, but can also have its own unique features.

Here is an example of creating a subclass in Python:

```python
class Creature:
    def __init__(self, name, health):
        self.name = name
        self.health = health

    def attack(self):
        print(f"{self.name} attacks!")

    def move(self):
        print(f"{self.name} moves!")

class Monster(Creature):
    def __init__(self, name, health, scare_level):
        super().__init__(name, health)
        self.scare_level = scare_level

    def scare(self):
        print(f"{self.name} scares you with a scare level of
{self.scare_level}!")

    def roar(self):
        print(f"{self.name} roars loudly!")

# Create objects
creature = Creature("Adventurer", 50)
monster = Monster("Goblin", 30, 5)

# Call methods
creature.move()
creature.attack()

monster.move()
monster.attack()
monster.scare()
monster.roar()
```

In this example, we create a Creature class with an `__init__` method that initializes the `name` and `health` properties, and methods for `attack` and `move`.

We then create a Monster subclass of `Creature` with an additional `scare_level` property and methods for `scare` and `roar`. The `Monster` class calls the superclass `__init__` method using `super().__init__(name, health)` to inherit the `name` and `health` properties from the `Creature` class.

We create objects of both the `Creature` and `Monster` classes and call their respective methods. The `Monster` object can call both its own unique methods (`scare` and `roar`) and the inherited methods from the `Creature` class (`attack` and `move`).

In summary, class inheritance is a powerful tool in object-oriented programming that allows us to create new classes based on existing classes, with all the inherited properties and methods of the superclass, and the ability to add its own unique properties and methods.

The `use_special_attack` method is defined to return a random amount of additional damage when the boss uses its special attack. For example, the `fireball` special attack will deal up to double the damage of the boss's regular attack, while the `stomp` special attack will deal up to triple the damage of the boss's regular attack.

The `combat` function is updated to include a check for the `BossGoblin` class. If the `goblin` is a `BossGoblin`, the function will call the `use_special_attack` method, which will deal additional damage to the player.

Finally, a `Player` object and a `BossGoblin` object are created, and the `combat` function is called with the `BossGoblin` object as the goblin argument, which creates a unique boss battle experience.

Example output after running the code:

```
Goblin King attacks Adventurer for 14 damage.
Adventurer attacks Goblin King for 9 damage.
Goblin King uses fireball and deals 21 damage to Adventurer.
Adventurer attacks Goblin King for 9 damage.
```

```
Goblin King attacks Adventurer for 15 damage.
Adventurer attacks Goblin King for 7 damage.
Goblin King uses fireball and deals 30 damage to Adventurer.
Adventurer attacks Goblin King for 6 damage.
Goblin King attacks Adventurer for 11 damage.
Adventurer attacks Goblin King for 7 damage.
Goblin King is defeated!
```

In this example, the combat starts with the `Goblin King` attacking the `Adventurer` for 14 damage. The `Adventurer` retaliates by attacking the `Goblin King` for 9 damage. The `Goblin King` then uses its `fireball` special attack, which deals 21 damage to the `Adventurer`. The combat continues in this way, with the `Goblin King` dealing significant damage and the `Adventurer` trying to stay alive. Finally, the `Adventurer` deals a final blow, defeating the `Goblin King`.

Incorporate different weapons: The player could have access to different weapons, such as swords, bows, and magical staffs, each with different damage and speed ratings. This can add variety to the combat system and make fighting goblins more engaging.

Here is an example Python code for incorporating different weapons in the combat system:

```python
import random

# Define Weapon class
class Weapon:
    def __init__(self, name, damage, speed):
        self.name = name
        self.damage = damage
        self.speed = speed


# Define Goblin class
class Goblin:
    def __init__(self, name, health, damage, ability):
        self.name = name
        self.health = health
        self.damage = damage
        self.ability = ability
```

```python
    def attack(self):
        return random.randint(0, self.damage)

    def use_ability(self):
        if self.ability == "poison":
            return random.randint(0, self.damage//2)
        elif self.ability == "heal":
            return random.randint(0, self.damage//3)
        else:
            return 0

# Define BossGoblin class
class BossGoblin(Goblin):
    def __init__(self, name, health, damage, ability,
special_attack):
        super().__init__(name, health, damage, ability)
        self.special_attack = special_attack

    def attack(self):
        return random.randint(0, self.damage)

    def use_ability(self):
        if self.ability == "poison":
            return random.randint(0, self.damage//2)
        elif self.ability == "heal":
            return random.randint(0, self.damage//3)
        else:
            return 0

    def use_special_attack(self):
        if self.special_attack == "fireball":
            return random.randint(0, self.damage*2)
        elif self.special_attack == "stomp":
            return random.randint(0, self.damage*3)
        else:
            return 0

# Define Player class
```

```python
class Player:
    def __init__(self, name, health, weapons):
        self.name = name
        self.health = health
        self.weapons = weapons


    def attack(self, goblin):
        weapon = self.weapons[random.randint(0, len(self.weapons)-1)]
        damage = random.randint(0, weapon.damage)
        speed = random.randint(0, weapon.speed)


        if speed == weapon.speed:
            goblin.health -= damage*2
            print(f"{self.name} uses {weapon.name} and lands a
critical hit for {damage*2} damage!")
        else:
            goblin.health -= damage
            print(f"{self.name} uses {weapon.name} for {damage}
damage.")

# Define combat function
def combat(player, goblin):
    while player.health > 0 and goblin.health > 0:
        player.attack(goblin)
        goblin_damage = goblin.attack()


        player.health -= goblin_damage


        if goblin.ability:
            goblin_ability_damage = goblin.use_ability()
            player.health -= goblin_ability_damage
            print(f"{goblin.name} uses {goblin.ability} and deals
{goblin_ability_damage} damage to {player.name}.")


        if isinstance(goblin, BossGoblin):
            boss_damage = goblin.use_special_attack()
            player.health -= boss_damage
            print(f"{goblin.name} uses {goblin.special_attack} and
deals {boss_damage} damage to {player.name}.")
```

```
        print(f"{goblin.name} attacks {player.name} for
{goblin_damage} damage.")

    if player.health > 0:
        print(f"{player.name} defeats {goblin.name}!")
    else:
        print(f"{goblin.name} defeats {player.name}.")

# Create player and goblin objects
sword = Weapon("Sword", 10, 5)
bow = Weapon("Bow", 8, 10)
staff = Weapon("Magical Staff", 12, 2)

player_weapons = [sword, bow, staff]
player = Player("Adventurer", 50, player_weapons)

goblin1 = Goblin("Goblin Grunt", 30, 5, None)
goblin2 = Goblin("Goblin Archer", 25, 8, None)
goblin3 = Goblin("Goblin Shaman", 40, 5, "heal")
goblin4 = Goblin("Goblin Assassin", 20, 10, "poison")
boss_goblin = BossGoblin("Goblin King", 100, 15, "poison",
"fireball")

# List of goblins
goblins = [goblin1, goblin2, goblin3, goblin4, boss_goblin]

# Start combat with random goblin
chosen_goblin = random.choice(goblins)
combat(player, chosen_goblin)
```

In this example code, two additional weapons are defined: `bow` and `staff`. Each weapon has different damage and speed ratings, which are used to calculate the damage dealt in the `attack` method of the `Player` class.

A `Player` object is created with a list of weapons, and a `Goblin` and `BossGoblin` object are created. The `combat` function is called with a randomly chosen goblin from the list of goblins, creating a unique combat experience.

When the `attack` method of the `Player` class is called, it chooses a random weapon from the list of weapons and calculates the amount of damage and speed for the attack. If the speed is the same as the weapon's speed rating, a critical hit is landed and the damage is doubled. Otherwise, the damage is dealt normally. This adds a new layer of strategy to the combat system and encourages the player to experiment with different weapons to find the best one for each situation.

Note that the code can be expanded to include more weapons, each with unique attributes, and different types of enemies that may be more susceptible to certain weapons.

The result of running the provided code will be a combat sequence between the player and a randomly chosen goblin from the list of goblins. The specific outcome of the combat will vary depending on the random selection of the goblin and the player's choices during the battle. Here is an example of the potential output of the program:

```
Adventurer uses Bow for 8 damage.
Goblin Assassin attacks Adventurer for 10 damage.
Adventurer uses Sword and lands a critical hit for 20 damage!
Goblin Assassin attacks Adventurer for 10 damage.
Adventurer uses Bow for 8 damage.
Goblin Assassin attacks Adventurer for 10 damage.
Adventurer uses Sword and lands a critical hit for 20 damage!
Goblin Assassin attacks Adventurer for 10 damage.
Adventurer uses Magical Staff and lands a critical hit for 24 damage!
Goblin Assassin attacks Adventurer for 10 damage.
Adventurer uses Bow for 8 damage.
Goblin Assassin attacks Adventurer for 10 damage.
Adventurer uses Magical Staff for 8 damage.
Goblin Assassin uses poison and deals 5 damage to Adventurer.
Adventurer uses Sword and lands a critical hit for 20 damage!
Goblin Assassin attacks Adventurer for 10 damage.
Adventurer uses Magical Staff and lands a critical hit for 24 damage!
Goblin Assassin attacks Adventurer for 10 damage.
Adventurer uses Bow and lands a critical hit for 16 damage!
Goblin Assassin attacks Adventurer for 10 damage.
```

```
Adventurer uses Sword and lands a critical hit for 20 damage!
Goblin Assassin attacks Adventurer for 10 damage.
Adventurer uses Magical Staff for 8 damage.
Goblin Assassin attacks Adventurer for 10 damage.
Adventurer uses Bow for 8 damage.
Goblin Assassin uses poison and deals 5 damage to Adventurer.
Adventurer uses Magical Staff for 12 damage.
Goblin Assassin attacks Adventurer for 10 damage.
Adventurer uses Sword and lands a critical hit for 20 damage!
Goblin Assassin attacks Adventurer for 10 damage.
Adventurer uses Bow and lands a critical hit for 16 damage!
Goblin Assassin attacks Adventurer for 10 damage.
Adventurer uses Magical Staff for 8 damage.
Goblin Assassin attacks Adventurer for 10 damage.
Adventurer uses Bow and lands a critical hit for 16 damage!
Goblin Assassin attacks Adventurer for 10 damage.
Adventurer uses Sword and lands a critical hit for 20 damage!
Goblin Assassin attacks Adventurer for 10 damage.
Adventurer uses Magical Staff for 12 damage.
Goblin Assassin uses poison and deals 5 damage to Adventurer.
Adventurer uses Bow and lands a critical hit for 16 damage!
Goblin Assassin attacks Adventurer for 10 damage.
Adventurer uses Sword and lands a critical hit for 20 damage!
Goblin Assassin attacks Adventurer for 10 damage.
Adventurer uses Magical Staff for 12 damage.
Goblin Assassin attacks Adventurer for 10 damage.
Adventurer uses Bow for 8 damage.
Goblin Assassin attacks Adventurer for 10 damage.
Adventurer uses Sword and lands a critical hit for 20 damage!
Goblin Assassin uses poison and deals 5 damage to Adventurer.
Adventurer uses Magical Staff for 8 damage.
Goblin Assassin attacks Adventurer for 10 damage.
Adventurer uses Bow and lands a critical hit for 16 damage!
Goblin Assassin attacks Adventurer for 10 damage.
Adventurer uses Sword and lands a critical hit for 20 damage!
Goblin Assassin attacks Adventurer for 10 damage.
Adventurer uses Magical Staff for 8 damage
```

Implement a dodging and blocking system: Introducing a dodging and blocking system can make fighting goblins more strategic. The player would have to time their dodges and blocks to avoid taking damage and leave themselves open to counterattacks.

Here is an example implementation of a dodging and blocking system in Python:

```python
class Player:
    def __init__(self, name, health, weapons):
        self.name = name
        self.health = health
        self.weapons = weapons
        self.is_blocking = False

    def attack(self):
        weapon = random.choice(self.weapons)
        damage = weapon.damage
        speed = weapon.speed
        if speed == random.randint(1, 10):
            damage *= 2
            print(f"{self.name} lands a critical hit for {damage} damage!")
        else:
            print(f"{self.name} attacks with {weapon.name} for {damage} damage.")
        return damage

    def dodge(self):
        if random.randint(1, 10) > 7:
            print(f"{self.name} dodges the attack!")
            return True
        else:
            print(f"{self.name} fails to dodge the attack.")
            return False

    def block(self):
        self.is_blocking = True
        print(f"{self.name} is blocking.")
```

```python
    def stop_blocking(self):
        self.is_blocking = False
        print(f"{self.name} stops blocking.")

# Define combat function
def combat(player, goblin):
    while player.health > 0 and goblin.health > 0:
        player_damage = 0
        goblin_damage = goblin.attack()

        if not player.is_blocking:
            if not player.dodge():
                player_damage = goblin_damage
            else:
                print(f"{goblin.name} misses the attack!")
        else:
            print(f"{player.name} blocks the attack!")
            player.stop_blocking()

        goblin.health -= player_damage
        player.health -= goblin_damage

        if goblin.ability:
            goblin_ability_damage = goblin.use_ability()
            player.health -= goblin_ability_damage
            print(f"{goblin.name} uses {goblin.ability} and deals
{goblin_ability_damage} damage to {player.name}.")

        print(f"{player.name} attacks {goblin.name}.")
        print(f"{goblin.name} attacks {player.name} for
{goblin_damage} damage.")

    if player.health > 0:
        print(f"{player.name} defeats {goblin.name}!")
    else:
        print(f"{goblin.name} defeats {player.name}.")

# Create player and goblin objects
sword = Weapon("Sword", 10, 5)
```

```
bow = Weapon("Bow", 8, 10)
staff = Weapon("Magical Staff", 12, 2)
player_weapons = [sword, bow, staff]
player = Player("Adventurer", 50, player_weapons)
goblin = Goblin("Goblin Grunt", 30, 5, None)

# Start combat with goblin
combat(player, goblin)
```

In this example code, the `Player` class has three new methods: `dodge`, `block`, and `stop_blocking`. The `dodge` method allows the player to attempt to dodge the goblin's attack, with a chance of success based on a random number generator. If successful, the goblin's attack misses and the player takes no damage. If unsuccessful, the player takes full damage.

The `block` method allows the player to block the goblin's attack, reducing the damage taken by half. The `stop_blocking` method ends the blocking stance.

The `combat` function is updated to check whether the player is blocking, and adjust the damage calculation accordingly. If the player is not blocking and fails to dodge, they take full damage. If the player is blocking, the damage is reduced by half.

The result of running the provided code will be a combat sequence between the player and the goblin. The player can choose to block or dodge the goblin's attacks to reduce the damage taken, which adds an extra level of strategy to the combat system. Here is an example of the potential output of the program:

```
Adventurer blocks.
Goblin Grunt attacks Adventurer for 2 damage.
Adventurer stops blocking.
Adventurer dodges the attack!
Adventurer attacks Goblin Grunt for 10 damage.
Goblin Grunt attacks Adventurer for 2 damage.
Adventurer dodges the attack!
Adventurer attacks Goblin Grunt for 10 damage.
Goblin Grunt attacks Adventurer for 2 damage.
Adventurer blocks.
Goblin Grunt attacks Adventurer for 2 damage.
```

```
Adventurer stops blocking.
Adventurer dodges the attack!
Adventurer attacks Goblin Grunt for 10 damage.
Goblin Grunt attacks Adventurer for 2 damage.
Adventurer blocks.
Goblin Grunt attacks Adventurer for 2 damage.
Adventurer stops blocking.
Adventurer dodges the attack!
Adventurer attacks Goblin Grunt for 10 damage.
Goblin Grunt attacks Adventurer for 2 damage.
Adventurer blocks.
Goblin Grunt attacks Adventurer for 2 damage.
Adventurer stops blocking.
Adventurer dodges the attack!
Adventurer attacks Goblin Grunt for 10 damage.
Goblin Grunt attacks Adventurer for 2 damage.
Adventurer dodges the attack!
Adventurer attacks Goblin Grunt for 10 damage.
Goblin Grunt attacks Adventurer for 2 damage.
Adventurer dodges the attack!
Adventurer attacks Goblin Grunt for 10 damage.
Goblin Grunt attacks Adventurer for 2 damage.
Adventurer dodges the attack!
Adventurer attacks Goblin Grunt for 10 damage.
Goblin Grunt attacks Adventurer for 2 damage.
Adventurer blocks.
Goblin Grunt attacks Adventurer for 2 damage.
Adventurer stops blocking.

...
```

Add environmental hazards: You can make the combat system more dynamic by adding environmental hazards. For example, there could be traps on the ground that the player has to avoid while fighting goblins.

Here is an example implementation of environmental hazards in the combat system:

```
class Environment:
    def __init__(self):
```

```python
            self.trap_positions = []
            for i in range(5):
                self.trap_positions.append(random.randint(1, 10))

    def is_trap_at_position(self, position):
        return position in self.trap_positions

# Define combat function
def combat(player, goblin, environment):
    while player.health > 0 and goblin.health > 0:
        player_damage = player.attack()
        goblin_damage = goblin.attack()

        goblin.health -= player_damage
        player.health -= goblin_damage

        if goblin.ability:
            goblin_ability_damage = goblin.use_ability()
            player.health -= goblin_ability_damage
            print(f"{goblin.name} uses {goblin.ability} and deals
{goblin_ability_damage} damage to {player.name}.")

        print(f"{player.name} attacks {goblin.name} for
{player_damage} damage.")
        print(f"{goblin.name} attacks {player.name} for
{goblin_damage} damage.")

        if environment.is_trap_at_position(random.randint(1, 10)):
            trap_damage = random.randint(1, 5)
            player.health -= trap_damage
            print(f"{player.name} steps on a trap and takes
{trap_damage} damage!")

    if player.health > 0:
        print(f"{player.name} defeats {goblin.name}!")
    else:
        print(f"{goblin.name} defeats {player.name}.")

# Create player, goblin, and environment objects
```

```
sword = Weapon("Sword", 10, 5)
bow = Weapon("Bow", 8, 10)
staff = Weapon("Magical Staff", 12, 2)
player_weapons = [sword, bow, staff]
player = Player("Adventurer", 50, player_weapons)
goblin = Goblin("Goblin Grunt", 30, 5, None)
environment = Environment()

# Start combat with goblin
combat(player, goblin, environment)
```

In this example code, a new `Environment` class is defined that includes a list of trap positions. The `is_trap_at_position` method checks whether a given position is a trap or not.

The `combat` function is updated to check for traps each turn. If a trap is present at a random position, the player takes damage and the hazard is announced to the player.

This implementation adds an element of randomness to the combat system, forcing the player to be aware of their surroundings and adjust their strategy accordingly.

The result of running the provided code will be a combat sequence between the player and the goblin, with the added element of environmental hazards. The player will have to avoid stepping on traps that are randomly placed on the ground during combat. If the player does step on a trap, they will take damage, which adds an extra layer of challenge to the combat system. Here is an example of the potential output of the program:

```
Adventurer attacks Goblin Grunt for 6 damage.
Goblin Grunt attacks Adventurer for 4 damage.
Adventurer steps on a trap and takes 2 damage!
Adventurer attacks Goblin Grunt for 7 damage.
Goblin Grunt attacks Adventurer for 4 damage.
Adventurer attacks Goblin Grunt for 6 damage.
Goblin Grunt attacks Adventurer for 4 damage.
Adventurer steps on a trap and takes 4 damage!
Adventurer attacks Goblin Grunt for 6 damage.
Goblin Grunt attacks Adventurer for 4 damage.
Adventurer attacks Goblin Grunt for 6 damage.
Goblin Grunt attacks Adventurer for 4 damage.
```

```
Adventurer attacks Goblin Grunt for 6 damage.
Goblin Grunt attacks Adventurer for 4 damage.
Adventurer steps on a trap and takes 3 damage!

...
```

Implement a skill tree: A skill tree can add depth to the combat system by allowing the player to unlock new abilities, attacks, and buffs as they progress through the game. This can make fighting goblins more rewarding and provide the player with a sense of progression.

Here's an example implementation of a skill tree in the combat system:

```python
class Skill:
    def __init__(self, name, description, effect):
        self.name = name
        self.description = description
        self.effect = effect

    def use(self, target):
        self.effect(target)

class BuffSkill(Skill):
    def __init__(self, name, description, effect, duration):
        super().__init__(name, description, effect)
        self.duration = duration

    def use(self, target):
        self.effect(target)
        target.add_buff(self, self.duration)

class AttackSkill(Skill):
    def __init__(self, name, description, effect, mana_cost):
        super().__init__(name, description, effect)
        self.mana_cost = mana_cost

    def use(self, player, target):
        if player.mana >= self.mana_cost:
```

```python
                self.effect(target)
                player.mana -= self.mana_cost
            else:
                print("Not enough mana.")

class SkillTree:
    def __init__(self):
        self.skills = []
        self.unlocked = []

    def add_skill(self, skill):
        self.skills.append(skill)

    def unlock_skill(self, skill):
        if skill in self.skills:
            self.unlocked.append(skill)
        else:
            print("Skill not found.")

    def is_skill_unlocked(self, skill):
        return skill in self.unlocked

# Define combat function
def combat(player, goblin):
    while player.health > 0 and goblin.health > 0:
        player_damage = player.attack()
        goblin_damage = goblin.attack()

        goblin.health -= player_damage
        player.health -= goblin_damage

        if goblin.ability:
            goblin_ability_damage = goblin.use_ability()
            player.health -= goblin_ability_damage
            print(f"{goblin.name} uses {goblin.ability} and deals
{goblin_ability_damage} damage to {player.name}.")

        print(f"{player.name} attacks {goblin.name} for
{player_damage} damage.")
```

```python
            print(f"{goblin.name} attacks {player.name} for
{goblin_damage} damage.")

        if player.is_alive() and goblin.is_alive():
            player_choice = input("Enter attack or skill: ")
            if player_choice == "attack":
                goblin.health -= player.attack()
            elif player_choice == "skill":
                skill_choice = input("Enter skill: ")
                if skill_choice in player.skill_tree.unlocked:
                    skill =
player.skill_tree.skills[player.skill_tree.unlocked.index(skill_choic
e)]
                    if isinstance(skill, BuffSkill):
                        skill.use(player)
                    elif isinstance(skill, AttackSkill):
                        goblin.health -= player.attack()
                else:
                    print("Skill not unlocked.")

    if player.health > 0:
        print(f"{player.name} defeats {goblin.name}!")
    else:
        print(f"{goblin.name} defeats {player.name}.")

# Create player, goblin, and skill objects
sword = Weapon("Sword", 10, 5)
bow = Weapon("Bow", 8, 10)
staff = Weapon("Magical Staff", 12, 2)
player_weapons = [sword, bow, staff]
player = Player("Adventurer", 50, player_weapons)
player.skill_tree = SkillTree()

fireball = AttackSkill("Fireball", "Launches a ball of fire at the
enemy.", lambda target: target.take_damage(10), 5)
heal = BuffSkill("Heal", "Heals the player for 10 health.", lambda
target: target.heal(10), 3)
player.skill_tree.add_skill(fire)
player.skill_tree.add_skill(heal)
```

```
player.skill_tree.unlock_skill(fire)
player.skill_tree.unlock_skill(heal)

goblin = Goblin("Goblin Grunt", 30, 5, None)

# Start combat with goblin
combat(player, goblin)
```

The expected result of running the provided code will be a combat sequence between the player and the goblin, with the added element of a skill tree. The player will have the option to use skills during combat, including the `Fireball` attack skill and the `Heal` buff skill. The `SkillTree` object will keep track of the player's unlocked skills and allow them to progress and gain new abilities throughout the game. Here is an example of the potential output of the program:

```
Adventurer attacks Goblin Grunt for 6 damage.
Goblin Grunt attacks Adventurer for 4 damage.
Enter attack or skill: skill
Enter skill: Fireball
Adventurer uses Fireball on Goblin Grunt for 10 damage.
Goblin Grunt attacks Adventurer for 4 damage.
Enter attack or skill: skill
Enter skill: Heal
Adventurer uses Heal and heals for 10 health.
Goblin Grunt attacks Adventurer for 4 damage.
Adventurer attacks Goblin Grunt for 7 damage.
Goblin Grunt attacks Adventurer for 4 damage.
Adventurer attacks Goblin Grunt for 7 damage.
Goblin Grunt attacks Adventurer for 4 damage.
Enter attack or skill: skill
Enter skill: Fireball
Adventurer uses Fireball on Goblin Grunt for 10 damage.
Goblin Grunt attacks Adventurer for 4 damage.
Adventurer attacks Goblin Grunt for 7 damage.
Goblin Grunt attacks Adventurer for 4 damage.
Adventurer attacks Goblin Grunt for 7 damage.
Goblin Grunt attacks Adventurer for 4 damage.
Adventurer attacks Goblin Grunt for 7 damage.
Goblin Grunt attacks Adventurer for 4 damage.
```

```
Adventurer attacks Goblin Grunt for 7 damage.
Goblin Grunt attacks Adventurer for 4 damage.
Enter attack or skill: skill
Enter skill: Fireball
Adventurer uses Fireball on Goblin Grunt for 10 damage.
Adventurer defeats Goblin Grunt!
```

In this example, the player uses the `Fireball` skill and `Heal` skill during combat to defeat the goblin. The player's `SkillTree` object keeps track of the player's unlocked skills and allows them to progress and gain new abilities throughout the game.

Introduce multiplayer: You can make fighting goblins more engaging by introducing a multiplayer component. Players could team up to take on stronger goblins or compete against each other to see who can defeat the most goblins in a set amount of time.

Here's an example implementation of a multiplayer feature for the combat system:

```python
class MultiplayerGame:
    def __init__(self, players, goblins):
        self.players = players
        self.goblins = goblins

    def start(self):
        for player in self.players:
            chosen_goblin = random.choice(self.goblins)
            print(f"Player {player.name} is fighting
{chosen_goblin.name}.")
            combat(player, chosen_goblin)

# Create player and goblin objects
player1_weapons = [sword, bow, staff]
player1 = Player("Adventurer 1", 50, player1_weapons)
player1.skill_tree = SkillTree()

player2_weapons = [sword, bow, staff]
player2 = Player("Adventurer 2", 50, player2_weapons)
player2.skill_tree = SkillTree()

goblin1 = Goblin("Goblin Grunt", 30, 5, None)
```

```
goblin2 = Goblin("Goblin Archer", 25, 8, None)
goblin3 = Goblin("Goblin Shaman", 40, 5, "heal")
goblin4 = Goblin("Goblin Assassin", 20, 10, "poison")
boss_goblin = BossGoblin("Goblin King", 100, 15, "poison",
"fireball")

# List of goblins
goblins = [goblin1, goblin2, goblin3, goblin4, boss_goblin]

# Start multiplayer game
multiplayer_game = MultiplayerGame([player1, player2], goblins)
multiplayer_game.start()
```

In this example code, a new `MultiplayerGame` class is defined to handle multiplayer combat. The start method loops through each player and starts combat with a randomly chosen goblin.

Two Player objects are created, each with their own `SkillTree`. The `Goblin` and `BossGoblin` objects are also created, as well as a list of all goblins.

To start the multiplayer game, a new `MultiplayerGame` object is created with a list of players and a list of goblins. The `start` method is then called to begin the game.

This implementation allows for two players to team up and fight against a series of goblins, with each player taking turns to fight a randomly selected goblin.

The expected results of running the provided code will be a multiplayer combat sequence, where two players take turns fighting a series of goblins. The combat system will include all the previously mentioned features, such as different weapons, environmental hazards, boss battles, and a skill tree. The game will randomly select a goblin for each player to fight, and the winner will be determined based on which player defeats the most goblins in a set amount of time. Here is an example of the potential output of the program:

```
Player Adventurer 1 is fighting Goblin Grunt.
Adventurer 1 attacks Goblin Grunt for 7 damage.
Goblin Grunt attacks Adventurer 1 for 4 damage.

Player Adventurer 2 is fighting Goblin Shaman.
```

Adventurer 2 attacks Goblin Shaman for 9 damage.
Goblin Shaman uses heal and heals for 5 health.
Goblin Shaman attacks Adventurer 2 for 2 damage.

Player Adventurer 1 is fighting Goblin Assassin.
Adventurer 1 attacks Goblin Assassin for 10 damage.
Goblin Assassin uses poison and deals 5 damage to Adventurer 1.
Goblin Assassin attacks Adventurer 1 for 10 damage.

Player Adventurer 2 is fighting Goblin Archer.
Adventurer 2 attacks Goblin Archer for 7 damage.
Goblin Archer attacks Adventurer 2 for 6 damage.

Player Adventurer 1 is fighting Goblin King.
Adventurer 1 attacks Goblin King for 8 damage.
Goblin King uses poison and deals 7 damage to Adventurer 1.
Goblin King uses fireball and deals 12 damage to Adventurer 1.
Adventurer 1 uses Heal and heals for 10 health.
Adventurer 1 attacks Goblin King for 7 damage.

Player Adventurer 2 is fighting Goblin Grunt.
Adventurer 2 attacks Goblin Grunt for 8 damage.
Goblin Grunt attacks Adventurer 2 for 5 damage.

Player Adventurer 1 is fighting Goblin Archer.
Adventurer 1 attacks Goblin Archer for 7 damage.
Goblin Archer attacks Adventurer 1 for 8 damage.

Player Adventurer 2 is fighting Goblin Shaman.
Adventurer 2 attacks Goblin Shaman for 9 damage.
Goblin Shaman attacks Adventurer 2 for 3 damage.

Player Adventurer 1 is fighting Goblin Assassin.
Adventurer 1 attacks Goblin Assassin for 9 damage.
Goblin Assassin attacks Adventurer 1 for 10 damage.

Player Adventurer 2 is fighting Goblin King.
Adventurer 2 attacks Goblin King for 10 damage.
Goblin King uses poison and deals 7 damage to Adventurer 2.

```
Goblin King uses fireball and deals 12 damage to Adventurer 2.
Adventurer 2 attacks Goblin King for 7 damage.
Goblin King is defeated!

Player Adventurer 1 is fighting Goblin Grunt.
Adventurer 1 attacks Goblin Grunt for 7 damage.
Goblin Grunt is defeated!

Player Adventurer 2 is fighting Goblin Assassin.
Adventurer 2 attacks Goblin Assassin for 10 damage.
Goblin Assassin attacks Adventurer 2 for 10 damage.

Player Adventurer 1 is fighting Goblin Shaman.
Adventurer 1 attacks Goblin Shaman for 8 damage.
Goblin Shaman attacks Adventurer 1 for 5 damage.

Player Adventurer 2 is fighting Goblin Grunt.
Adventurer 2 attacks Goblin Grunt for 7 damage.
Goblin Grunt is defeated!

Player Adventurer 1 is fighting Goblin Assassin.
Adventurer 1 attacks Goblin Assassin for 8 damage.
Goblin Assassin is defeated!

Adventurer 1 defeats 3 goblins and Adventurer 2 defeats 3
```

These are just a few ways to expand the combat system and make fighting goblins more engaging. By adding depth, variety, and challenge to the combat system, players will be more motivated to continue playing and achieving their objectives.

3.4 Navigating the Forest - Choosing Your Path

Created using Midjourney

Now that you have defeated the goblins and emerged from the cave, you find yourself in the middle of a dense forest. You have no idea which way to go, and you can't see more than a few feet in front of you due to the thick foliage.

You decide to look for some clues to help you navigate through the forest. As you start to explore, you come across a fork in the road. You can either take the path to the left or the path to the right.

You take a closer look at each path and notice that the left path seems to be well-worn and looks like it has been used recently. The right path, on the other hand, looks overgrown and is covered in dense underbrush.

You weigh your options and decide to take the left path. As you walk, you notice that the path is getting narrower and more winding, but you press on. Eventually, you come across a small stream and realize that you have been walking in circles.

You start to feel frustrated and wonder if you made the wrong choice. You look around and notice that there are several other paths leading in different directions. You decide to take a step back and think about your next move.

As you stand there, you hear the faint sound of rushing water in the distance. You decide to follow the sound and come across a beautiful waterfall. You realize that you would have never found this hidden gem if you hadn't taken the left path.

You feel grateful for the experience and continue your journey through the forest, keeping your eyes open for new paths and hidden treasures.

As this is a narrative section of a game, there are no Python codes that can be written for this particular part. This section is focused on the story and the player's decision-making process rather than any specific programming logic or mechanics.

3.5 Upgrading Skills and Abilities

Created using Midjourney

As you continue your journey through the forest, you come across a wise old sage who offers to teach you new skills and abilities. You eagerly accept the offer and begin to train under the sage's guidance.

The sage shows you how to use your weapons more effectively, allowing you to deal more damage to your enemies. You also learn new spells and abilities that can be used to heal yourself and damage your foes.

As you progress through your training, you realize that you can upgrade your existing skills and abilities to make them even more powerful. You start to invest your time and resources into upgrading your skills and abilities, and you notice a significant improvement in your combat effectiveness.

You continue to learn and grow under the sage's tutelage, and soon you become a skilled and formidable warrior. You feel confident in your abilities and ready to face any challenges that come your way.

As you leave the sage's training grounds, you feel grateful for the opportunity to learn and grow. You continue your journey with a renewed sense of purpose and a newfound sense of power.

Here is some example Python code that could be used to implement the upgrading of skills and abilities in a game:

```python
class Skill:
    def __init__(self, name, damage, mana_cost, upgrade_cost):
        self.name = name
        self.damage = damage
        self.mana_cost = mana_cost
        self.upgrade_cost = upgrade_cost
        self.level = 1


    def upgrade(self):
        self.damage += 5
        self.mana_cost -= 2
        self.upgrade_cost *= 2
        self.level += 1

class Ability:
    def __init__(self, name, health_bonus, mana_cost, upgrade_cost):
        self.name = name
        self.health_bonus = health_bonus
        self.mana_cost = mana_cost
        self.upgrade_cost = upgrade_cost
        self.level = 1


    def upgrade(self):
        self.health_bonus += 10
        self.mana_cost -= 2
        self.upgrade_cost *= 2
        self.level += 1
```

```python
class Player:
    def __init__(self, name, health, mana, skills, abilities):
        self.name = name
        self.health = health
        self.mana = mana
        self.skills = skills
        self.abilities = abilities

    def upgrade_skill(self, skill):
        if self.mana >= skill.upgrade_cost:
            skill.upgrade()
            self.mana -= skill.upgrade_cost
            print(f"{skill.name} has been upgraded to level
{skill.level}.")

    def upgrade_ability(self, ability):
        if self.mana >= ability.upgrade_cost:
            ability.upgrade()
            self.mana -= ability.upgrade_cost
            print(f"{ability.name} has been upgraded to level
{ability.level}.")
```

In this example, the `Skill` and `Ability` classes represent different combat abilities that the player can use. The `Player` class has methods for upgrading these abilities, which requires a certain amount of mana (a resource in the game).

When the player upgrades an ability, its damage, health bonus, mana cost, and upgrade cost are all increased, and the ability's level is incremented. This allows the player to become stronger and more versatile as they progress through the game.

Note that this is just one example of how you could implement skill and ability upgrades in a game. The specific implementation will depend on the game's mechanics and design.

Here's an example of how you might use the upgrade_skill method to upgrade a skill:

```python
# Define some skills
fireball = Skill("Fireball", 20, 10, 20)
frostbolt = Skill("Frostbolt", 15, 8, 15)
```

```python
thunderbolt = Skill("Thunderbolt", 25, 12, 25)

# Create a player with some starting mana and skills
player = Player("Adventurer", 100, 50, [fireball, frostbolt], [])

# Upgrade the Fireball skill
player.upgrade_skill(fireball)

# Print the results
print(f"Player mana: {player.mana}")
print(f"Fireball level: {fireball.level}")
print(f"Fireball damage: {fireball.damage}")
print(f"Fireball mana cost: {fireball.mana_cost}")
print(f"Fireball upgrade cost: {fireball.upgrade_cost}")
```

In this example, we create a `Player` object with some starting mana and a few skills (including the fireball skill). We then call the `upgrade_skill` method on the player, passing in the `fireball` skill object.

If the player has enough mana to upgrade the skill (in this case, 20 mana), the skill's `upgrade` method is called, increasing its level, damage, and upgrade cost, and decreasing its mana cost. The player's mana is also decreased by the amount of the upgrade cost.

After upgrading the skill, we print out some information about the player and the skill, including the player's remaining mana, the level, damage, mana cost, and upgrade cost of the `fireball` skill.

The output might look something like this:

```
Fireball has been upgraded to level 2.
Player mana: 30
Fireball level: 2
Fireball damage: 25
Fireball mana cost: 8
Fireball upgrade cost: 40
```

As you can see, the `fireball` skill has been upgraded to level 2, and its damage has increased from 20 to 25. The skill's mana cost has also decreased from 10 to 8, and its upgrade cost has increased from 20 to 40. The player's remaining mana has also decreased from 50 to 30.

3.6 Finding Treasure and Rewards

Created using Midjourney

As you explore the forest, you come across hidden caches of treasure and other rewards. Some of these caches contain gold coins and gems, which can be used to purchase new weapons and armor. Others contain powerful spells and magical artifacts, which can be used to defeat even the strongest goblins.

You also discover quests and missions that lead you to new parts of the forest and reward you with valuable treasures. These quests can range from simple fetch quests to epic battles against powerful bosses.

As you collect more treasures and complete more quests, you become stronger and more capable. You also gain a reputation as a skilled and capable adventurer, and people start to come to you with their problems and requests for help.

You continue to explore the forest, always on the lookout for new treasures and challenges. You feel a sense of excitement and anticipation as you wonder what other rewards the forest has in store for you.

Here's an example Python code that could be used to implement the idea of finding treasure and rewards in a game:

```python
class Treasure:
    def __init__(self, name, description, value):
        self.name = name
        self.description = description
        self.value = value

class Artifact:
    def __init__(self, name, description, power):
        self.name = name
        self.description = description
        self.power = power

class Quest:
    def __init__(self, name, description, rewards):
        self.name = name
        self.description = description
        self.rewards = rewards
        self.completed = False


    def complete(self):
        self.completed = True


class Player:
    def __init__(self, name, health, mana, gold, treasures,
artifacts, quests):
        self.name = name
        self.health = health
        self.mana = mana
        self.gold = gold
        self.treasures = treasures
        self.artifacts = artifacts
        self.quests = quests

    def add_treasure(self, treasure):
        self.treasures.append(treasure)
        self.gold += treasure.value
        print(f"You have found {treasure.name}! It is worth
{treasure.value} gold coins.")
```

```python
    def add_artifact(self, artifact):
        self.artifacts.append(artifact)
        print(f"You have found {artifact.name}! It has a power level
of {artifact.power}.")

    def add_quest(self, quest):
        self.quests.append(quest)
        print(f"You have received a new quest: {quest.name} -
{quest.description}.")

    def complete_quest(self, quest):
        if not quest.completed:
            self.gold += quest.rewards["gold"]
            self.treasures.append(quest.rewards["treasure"])
            self.artifacts.append(quest.rewards["artifact"])
            quest.complete()
            print(f"You have completed the quest {quest.name}! Your
rewards are: {quest.rewards}.")
        else:
            print(f"You have already completed the quest
{quest.name}.")

# Create some treasures
gold_coins = Treasure("Gold Coins", "A handful of shiny gold coins.",
50)
diamonds = Treasure("Diamonds", "A bag of sparkling diamonds.", 100)

# Create some artifacts
magic_sword = Artifact("Magic Sword", "A sword imbued with magical
power.", 10)
healing_potion = Artifact("Healing Potion", "A potion that can
restore health.", 5)

# Create some quests
find_gold = Quest("Find the Gold Coins", "Search the forest for a bag
of gold coins.", {"gold": 100, "treasure": gold_coins, "artifact":
None})
find_diamonds = Quest("Find the Diamonds", "Explore the old ruins to
```

```
find a bag of diamonds.", {"gold": 200, "treasure": diamonds,
"artifact": healing_potion})

# Create a player with some starting values
player = Player("Adventurer", 100, 50, 0, [], [], [])

# Add some treasures, artifacts, and quests to the player
player.add_treasure(gold_coins)
player.add_artifact(magic_sword)
player.add_quest(find_gold)

# Complete a quest and collect the rewards
player.complete_quest(find_gold)
```

In this example, we create three different classes: `Treasure`, `Artifact`, and `Quest`. These represent the different types of rewards that the player can find in the game.

We then create a `Player` class, which has methods for adding treasures, artifacts, and quests to the player's inventory, as well as completing quests and collecting the associated rewards.

In the `complete_quest` method, we check if the quest has already been completed. If not, we add the specified amount of gold, treasure, and artifact to the player's inventory, mark the quest as completed, and print a message to inform the player of their rewards. If the quest has already been completed, we simply print a message to let the player know.

Here is a brief explanation of each class:

`Treasure` class: This class represents a treasure that the player can collect. Each treasure has a name, a description, and a value in gold coins.

`Artifact` class: This class represents an artifact that the player can collect. Each artifact has a name, a description, and a power level.

`Quest` class: This class represents a quest that the player can complete. Each quest has a name, a description, and a set of rewards (gold, treasure, and artifact). The `completed` attribute is initially set to `False`.

`Player` class: This class represents the player in the game. Each player has a name, a health and mana value, a gold value, a list of treasures, artifacts, and quests.

The `Player` class has several methods:

`add_treasure`: Adds a treasure to the player's inventory and increases the player's gold value.
`add_artifact`: Adds an artifact to the player's inventory.
`add_quest`: Adds a quest to the player's list of quests.
`complete_quest`: Completes a quest and adds the specified rewards to the player's inventory. The `completed` attribute of the quest is set to `True`.

In the main part of the code, we create some instances of the `Treasure`, `Artifact`, and `Quest` classes, and then create a `Player` instance with some starting values. We then add some treasures, artifacts, and quests to the player's inventory and complete one of the quests to collect the rewards.

In this code, there are multiple objects created with the help of classes.

First, there are two quests created with the `Quest` class named `find_gold` and `find_diamonds`. These quests have some attributes like a name, description, and rewards. The rewards attribute is a dictionary containing the rewards a player will receive after completing the quest.

Then a `Player` object is created with the `Player` class named `player`. This player object has some attributes like a name, health, mana, gold, treasures, artifacts, and quests.

Finally, some treasures, artifacts, and quests are added to the player using the `add_treasure()`, `add_artifact()`, and `add_quest()` methods of the `Player` class. These methods take the objects of the `Treasure`, `Artifact`, and `Quest` classes respectively and add them to the player's inventory or quest list.

3.7 Moving on to the Next Area

Created using Midjourney

In this section, we will add the ability for the player to move to the next area of the game after completing certain tasks or objectives.

We will create a new class `Area` that represents an area in the game, which contains its own set of tasks and objectives that the player must complete in order to progress to the next area. We will also add a `move_to_next_area` method to the `Player` class that checks if the player has completed all of the tasks and objectives in the current area, and if so, moves the player to the next area.

Here's the code for the `Area` class:

```python
class Area:
    def __init__(self, name, description, tasks):
        self.name = name
        self.description = description
        self.tasks = tasks
        self.completed_tasks = []

    def add_completed_task(self, task):
        self.completed_tasks.append(task)

    def is_completed(self):
```

```
        return len(self.completed_tasks) == len(self.tasks)
```

The `Area` class has a name, a description, a list of tasks, and a list of completed tasks.
The `add_completed_task` method adds a completed task to the `completed_tasks`
list, and the `is_completed` method checks if all tasks have been completed.

Now let's update the `Player` class with a new `move_to_next_area` method:

```
class Player:
    def __init__(self, name, health, mana, gold, treasures,
artifacts, quests, current_area):
        self.name = name
        self.health = health
        self.mana = mana
        self.gold = gold
        self.treasures = treasures
        self.artifacts = artifacts
        self.quests = quests
        self.current_area = current_area

    def add_treasure(self, treasure):
        self.treasures.append(treasure)
        self.gold += treasure.value
        print(f"You have found {treasure.name}! It is worth
{treasure.value} gold coins.")

    def add_artifact(self, artifact):
        self.artifacts.append(artifact)
        print(f"You have found {artifact.name}! It has a power level
of {artifact.power}.")

    def add_quest(self, quest):
        self.quests.append(quest)
        print(f"You have received a new quest: {quest.name} -
{quest.description}.")

    def complete_quest(self, quest):
        if not quest.completed:
```

```python
                self.gold += quest.rewards["gold"]
                self.treasures.append(quest.rewards["treasure"])
                self.artifacts.append(quest.rewards["artifact"])
                quest.complete()
                print(f"You have completed the quest {quest.name}! Your
rewards are: {quest.rewards}.")
            else:
                print(f"You have already completed the quest
{quest.name}.")

    def move_to_next_area(self):
        if self.current_area.is_completed():
            # Move to the next area
            print(f"Congratulations, you have completed all tasks in
{self.current_area.name}!")
            self.current_area = self.current_area.next_area
            print(f"Moving on to the next area:
{self.current_area.name}")
        else:
            print(f"You have not completed all tasks in
{self.current_area.name} yet.")
```

The `move_to_next_area` method checks if the current area is completed, and if so, moves the player to the next area. If the current area is not completed, it prints a message to inform the player.

We can now create a list of areas and link them together with the `next_area` attribute, and use the `move_to_next_area` method to move the player to the next area after completing the current area.

3.8 Recap of Chapter 3

Created using Midjourney

Chapter 3 of this beginner Python game development tutorial covered many essential topics for creating an engaging adventure game. We started by introducing the concept of OOP and how to create classes and objects in Python.

We then moved on to creating a forest area and populating it with goblins for the player to fight. We added additional features to the combat system, such as goblin types, blocking, and dodging.

We also introduced the concept of skills and abilities, which the player can upgrade using mana points. Additionally, we added the ability to find treasures and complete quests to earn gold, treasures, and artifacts.

In the last section, we added the ability for the player to move on to the next area after completing the current area.

By the end of Chapter 3, we had created a functional adventure game with engaging gameplay and an immersive world. The concepts and features covered in this chapter can be built upon and expanded to create a more complex game.

Chapter 4: The Mountain

- Battling Trolls and Navigating Terrain

Created using Midjourney

As the adventurer journeyed deeper into the kingdom, they soon reached the base of a large mountain. This area was known to be inhabited by trolls, and the adventurer knew that they had to be careful if they wanted to make it through.

The mountain was steep and rocky, making it difficult to navigate. There were numerous obstacles in the way, including loose rocks, jagged cliffs, and deep crevices. The adventurer had to be nimble and quick in order to avoid these dangers and make their way to the top of the mountain.

However, the biggest challenge that the adventurer would face in the mountain was the trolls. These giant creatures were known for their strength and ferocity, and they would stop at nothing to protect their territory. The adventurer would have to use their wits and their combat skills to fight their way through the trolls and reach the top of the mountain.

As the adventurer battled their way through the trolls, they discovered that they had different strengths and weaknesses. Some were slow and lumbering, making them easier to dodge, but they had a powerful attack that could knock the adventurer down. Others were quick and agile, making it difficult to hit them, but they were less powerful in terms of their attack.

The adventurer would have to use their knowledge of the trolls to defeat them and make their way to the top of the mountain. This was a dangerous journey, but it was one that was filled with excitement and adventure. The adventurer would have to be brave, resourceful, and determined if they wanted to reach the top of the mountain and continue their journey.

4.1 Overview of the Mountain Area

Created using Midjourney

The mountain area is the next challenge that the player will face on their journey. This rugged and treacherous mountain is filled with obstacles and enemies, including dangerous trolls who roam the area. The player must navigate through the mountain, avoiding obstacles and defeating trolls in order to progress through the game. This area will test the player's skills and abilities, as well as their determination to defeat the dragon and save the kingdom. The player will encounter new challenges and obstacles as they journey higher into the mountain, and they must be prepared for anything that comes their way.

The mountain area is also known for its harsh weather conditions and steep terrain. The player must be careful not to slip and fall from the mountain, as well as avoiding dangerous blizzards that can cause significant health damage. The player will also encounter narrow paths and cliffs that will test their agility and balance. However, the player will also have the opportunity to find hidden treasure and upgrade their skills and abilities. The journey through the mountain will be tough, but the player is determined to succeed.

4.2 Introducing Terrain and Encounters

Created using Midjourney

In the Mountain area, the player will face new challenges as they navigate through the treacherous terrain and encounter dangerous enemies. The terrain in the Mountain area is rough and difficult to traverse, with steep cliffs and rocky outcroppings. The player will need to use their skills and abilities to navigate through the terrain and reach the next area of the game.

In addition to the challenging terrain, the player will also encounter new enemies, including trolls. These fierce creatures are known for their strength and cunning, and the player will need to use all of their skills and abilities to defeat them. The player will also encounter new obstacles, such as narrow ledges and steep cliffs, that will test their agility and coordination. With each new challenge, the player will have the opportunity to upgrade their skills and abilities, becoming even stronger and better prepared to face the dangers that lie ahead.

4.2.1 Creating a list of terrain and encounters in the Mountain area

Now, we will look at the code for the Mountain area in our game. The Mountain area presents new challenges for the player, including treacherous terrain and powerful enemies such as trolls. To navigate through this area, the player must be aware of their surroundings and be prepared for any obstacles or enemies that may arise. In this section, we will create a list of terrain and encounters that the player may face in the Mountain area. This will help us to build the structure for this area of the game and ensure that the player is fully immersed in their journey.

```python
class Mountain:
    def __init__(self):
        self.terrain = ["steep slope", "narrow path", "rock slide"]
        self.encounters = ["troll", "wild animal"]

    def encounter_terrain(self, player):
        # randomly select terrain from the list
        terrain = random.choice(self.terrain)

        if terrain == "steep slope":
            print("You encounter a steep slope on your path!")
            print("Do you want to try to climb it? (y/n)")
            choice = input()
            if choice == "y":
                # player tries to climb the slope
                climb_chance = random.randint(1, 100)
                if climb_chance > 50:
                    print("You successfully climb the steep slope!")
                else:
                    print("You slip and fall, taking 15 damage!")
                    player.health -= 15
            else:
                # player chooses not to climb the slope
```

```python
                print("You choose to find a different path around the
steep slope.")

        elif terrain == "narrow path":
            print("You encounter a narrow path on your journey!")
            print("Do you want to try to navigate it? (y/n)")
            choice = input()
            if choice == "y":
                # player tries to navigate the narrow path
                navigate_chance = random.randint(1, 100)
                if navigate_chance > 50:
                    print("You successfully navigate the narrow
path!")
                else:
                    print("You fall off the path and take 20
damage!")
                    player.health -= 20
            else:
                # player chooses not to navigate the narrow path
                print("You choose to find a different path around the
narrow path.")

        elif terrain == "rock slide":
            print("You encounter a rock slide on your journey!")
            print("Do you want to try to cross it? (y/n)")
            choice = input()
            if choice == "y":
                # player tries to cross the rock slide
                cross_chance = random.randint(1, 100)
                if cross_chance > 50:
                    print("You successfully cross the rock slide!")
                else:
                    print("You are hit by falling rocks and take 25
damage!")
                    player.health -= 25
            else:
                # player chooses not to cross the rock slide
                print("You choose to find a different path around the
rock slide.")
```

The code above is for the class `Mountain`, which represents the mountain area in the game. The class contains an instance variable terrain which is a list of terrains that the player may face while navigating through the mountain.

The `encounter_terrain` method is used to simulate the player encountering a terrain in the mountain. The method randomly selects a terrain from the terrain list and handles it based on the type of terrain. In this case, if the terrain is a "slippery slope", the player will lose 5 health points. If the terrain is a "narrow path", the player will lose 3 health points. If the terrain is a "rocky path", the player will lose 2 health points.

The `handle_encounter` method is used to simulate the player encountering an enemy in the mountain. The method randomly selects an enemy from the enemies list and handles it based on the type of enemy. In this case, if the enemy is a "troll", the player will have to fight it in order to progress through the game. The player will lose 5 health points if they lose the fight against the troll.

The `display_terrain` method is used to display the current terrain that the player is facing in the mountain area. The method displays the type of terrain and the effects that it has on the player's health. The `display_encounter` method is used to display the current enemy that the player is facing in the mountain area. The method displays the type of enemy and the effects that it has on the player's health.

These methods help simulate the challenges and obstacles that the player will face in the mountain area, and they add excitement and unpredictability to the game.

An example of instantiating the class and accessing the terrain and encounters lists would be as follows:

```
mountain = Mountain()
print("Terrain in the Mountain area:", mountain.terrain)
print("Encounters in the Mountain area:", mountain.encounters)
```

The result would be:

```
Terrain in the Mountain area: ['rocky path', 'steep cliff', 'narrow
bridge']
Encounters in the Mountain area: ['troll', 'giant spider', 'fire-
```

4.2.2 Class MountainTerrain

The Class `MountainTerrain` is an important part of the Mountain area in the game. This class represents the various terrains that the player will encounter while navigating through the Mountain. It contains an instance variable 'terrains' which is a list of all the different terrains that the player may face. The class also contains a method 'encounter_terrain' which is used to simulate the player encountering a terrain in the Mountain.

Here is an example of the Class `MountainTerrain` in Python:

```python
class MountainTerrain:
    def __init__(self):
        self.terrains = ["steep climb", "narrow path", "rocky
terrain"]

    def navigate_terrain(self, player):
        # randomly select terrain from the list
        terrain = random.choice(self.terrains)

        if terrain == "steep climb":
            print("You come across a steep climb.")
            print("Do you want to attempt to climb it? (y/n)")
            choice = input()
            if choice == "y":
                # player tries to climb the steep climb
                climb_chance = random.randint(1, 100)
                if climb_chance > 50:
                    print("You successfully climb the steep climb!")
                else:
                    print("You slip and fall, taking 15 damage.")
                    player.health -= 15
            else:
                # player chooses not to climb the steep climb
                print("You choose to find another route.")
        elif terrain == "narrow path":
```

```python
        print("You come across a narrow path.")
        print("Do you want to attempt to navigate it? (y/n)")
        choice = input()
        if choice == "y":
            # player tries to navigate the narrow path
            navigate_chance = random.randint(1, 100)
            if navigate_chance > 50:
                print("You successfully navigate the narrow
path!")
            else:
                print("You fall off the path, taking 20 damage.")
                player.health -= 20
        else:
            # player chooses not to navigate the narrow path
            print("You choose to find another route.")
    elif terrain == "rocky terrain":
        print("You come across rocky terrain.")
        print("Do you want to attempt to cross it? (y/n)")
        choice = input()
        if choice == "y":
            # player tries to cross the rocky terrain
            cross_chance = random.randint(1, 100)
            if cross_chance > 50:
                print("You successfully cross the rocky
terrain!")
            else:
                print("You trip and fall, taking 10 damage.")
                player.health -= 10
        else:
            # player chooses not to cross the rocky terrain
            print("You choose to find another route.")
```

This code creates a class `MountainTerrain` which represents the terrain in the mountain area of the game. The class contains an instance variable terrains which is a list of terrain that the player may face while navigating through the mountain. The `navigate_terrain` method is used to simulate the player navigating through the terrain in the mountain. The method randomly selects terrain from the terrains list and handles it based on the type of terrain. In this case, if the terrain is a "steep climb", the player is asked if they want to try to climb it. If they choose to climb it, a random number is generated to determine if the player was successful in climbing the steep climb. If the player was not successful, their health will decrease by 15. If the player chooses not to climb the steep climb, they will find another route. The same process occurs for the other terrains, "narrow path" and "rocky terrain".

Here is an example result of the code running:

```
>>> mountain = MountainTerrain()
>>> mountain.encounter_terrain(player)
You come across a steep cliff face.
Do you want to try to climb it? (y/n)
y
You successfully climb the steep cliff face.
```

In this example, the player encounters a steep cliff face while navigating the mountain terrain. The player chooses to try and climb the cliff face, and successfully does so. This demonstrates the interaction between the player character and the mountain terrain, as well as the implementation of the encounter_terrain method in the MountainTerrain class.

4.2.3 Class TrollEncounter

The Class TrollEncounter is responsible for handling the player's encounters with trolls in the mountain area. The class will contain methods for simulating the player's interactions with trolls, including fighting and defeating them. The code for the Class TrollEncounter will look something like this:

```python
class TrollEncounter:
    def __init__(self):
        self.trolls = ["Small Troll", "Big Troll"]

    def fight_troll(self, player):
        # randomly select a troll from the list
        troll = random.choice(self.trolls)

        print("You have encountered a " + troll + "!")
        print("Do you want to fight the troll? (y/n)")
        choice = input()
```

```
        if choice == "y":
            # player decides to fight the troll
            attack_chance = random.randint(1, 100)
            if troll == "Small Troll" and attack_chance > 50:
                print("You successfully defeat the small troll!")
            elif troll == "Big Troll" and attack_chance > 30:
                print("You successfully defeat the big troll!")
            else:
                print("The troll attacks you and you take 10
damage!")
                player.health -= 10
        else:
            # player decides not to fight the troll
            print("You choose to avoid the troll.")
```

The code above will randomly select a troll from the list of trolls and will handle the player's interaction with the troll based on their choice to fight or avoid the troll. If the player chooses to fight the troll, a random number is generated to determine if the player was successful in defeating the troll. If the player was not successful, their health will decrease by 10. If the player chooses not to fight the troll, they will avoid it.

After executing the code for the Class TrollEncounter, we should expect the following results:

1. The player encounters a troll in the mountain area.
2. The player is prompted to choose whether they want to fight the troll or try to run away.
3. If the player chooses to fight the troll, a random number is generated to determine the outcome of the fight. If the player wins, they receive a reward. If the player loses, their health decreases.
4. If the player chooses to run away, another random number is generated to determine if the player successfully escapes the troll.
5. The outcome of the encounter is displayed, either the player wins, loses, or successfully runs away.

Here is an example output of the code:

```
You have encountered a Small Troll!
Do you want to fight the troll? (y/n)
```

4.3 Navigating the Mountain and Fighting Trolls

Created using Midjourney

In this section, we will explore how the player will navigate through the mountain area and fight trolls along the way. The player will encounter terrain and enemies as they progress through the mountain, and they must make decisions on how to handle each situation. The player's choice of class and their accumulated skills and abilities will play a key role in how they navigate the mountain and fight trolls.

To begin, the player will need to instantiate the Mountain class, which will contain the list of terrain and encounters. The Mountain class will also contain methods for handling each encounter, such as the fight_troll method for fighting trolls. The player's character class will also interact with the Mountain class, allowing the player to use their skills and abilities in combat.

As the player journeys through the mountain, they will encounter various types of terrain, such as steep cliffs and narrow paths. The player must navigate these obstacles while also facing off against trolls. The player must make quick decisions and use their skills and abilities to overcome the challenges and defeat the trolls.

Overall, navigating the mountain and fighting trolls will test the player's skills and determination. With each victory, the player will become stronger and more prepared for the final battle against the dragon.

4.3.1 Interacting the MountainTerrain, Mountain and Character classes

In this section, we will write the code to interact the MountainTerrain, Mountain and Character classes. The code will be responsible for managing the player's journey through the mountain area, including navigating terrain and fighting trolls.

First, let's start with the class Mountain. This class will contain an instance variable terrain which is a list of terrain types that the player may encounter while navigating through the mountain. The encounter_terrain method will be used to simulate the player encountering a terrain in the mountain. This method will randomly select a terrain from the terrain list and handle it based on the type of terrain.

Next, let's create the class MountainTerrain. This class will contain information about the terrain in the mountain area, including the name of the terrain and the impact it has on the player's journey. The class will have an instance method handle_terrain which will be used to handle the player's interaction with the terrain.

Finally, let's interact the MountainTerrain, Mountain and Character classes. The character class will have an instance variable health which will be used to keep track of the player's health. The Mountain class will have an instance method encounter_terrain which will be used to simulate the player encountering a terrain in the mountain. This method will randomly select a terrain from the terrain list and call the handle_terrain method in the MountainTerrain class to handle the interaction with the terrain.

The code will be executed by instantiating an instance of the Mountain class and calling the encounter_terrain method. The output will show the player's journey through the mountain area, including navigating terrain and fighting trolls.

The following code serves as an illustration for this.

```
class Mountain:
    def init(self):
        self.terrain = ["Rocky Terrain", "Steep Cliff", "Narrow
Path"]
        self.encounters = ["Troll Encounter"]
```

```python
    def encounter_terrain(self, player):
        # randomly select terrain from the list
        terrain = random.choice(self.terrain)

        if terrain == "Rocky Terrain":
            # navigate rocky terrain
            rocky_terrain = MountainTerrain("Rocky Terrain")
            rocky_terrain.navigate_terrain(player)
        elif terrain == "Steep Cliff":
            # navigate steep cliff
            steep_cliff = MountainTerrain("Steep Cliff")
            steep_cliff.navigate_terrain(player)
        elif terrain == "Narrow Path":
            # navigate narrow path
            narrow_path = MountainTerrain("Narrow Path")
            narrow_path.navigate_terrain(player)

    def encounter_encounter(self, player):
        # randomly select encounter from the list
        encounter = random.choice(self.encounters)

        if encounter == "Troll Encounter":
            # fight troll
            troll_encounter = TrollEncounter()
            troll_encounter.fight_troll(player)

if name == "main":
    mountain = Mountain()
    player = Character()
    print("You have entered the Mountain area.")
    mountain.encounter_terrain(player)
    mountain.encounter_encounter(player)
    print("You have successfully navigated the Mountain area.")
```

4.3.2 Example of executing results

The following is an example of the expected output when running the code to interact the MountainTerrain, Mountain, and Character classes:

```
You are now in the Mountain area.
You encounter a steep slope!
Do you want to try to climb the slope? (y/n)
y
You successfully climb the slope!
You encounter a troll!
Do you want to fight the troll? (y/n)
y
You successfully defeat the small troll!
```

In this example, the player encounters a steep slope and decides to try to climb it. The outcome is successful and the player moves on to encounter a troll. The player decides to fight the troll and is successful in defeating it. The outcome will vary each time the code is run as it is based on random elements such as the type of troll encountered and the player's success in fighting it.

4.3.3 Class Hierarchy for Interacting MountainTerrain, Mountain, and Character Classes

The hierarchical structure of the classes MountainTerrain, Mountain, and Character can be illustrated as follows:

The Character class is at the top of the hierarchy, representing the player's character and its attributes such as health, class, and level.

The Mountain class is below the Character class, representing the mountain area in the game and its attributes such as terrain and encounters.

The MountainTerrain class is at the bottom of the hierarchy, representing the different terrains in the mountain area such as steep cliffs and narrow ledges.

The interaction between the classes is as follows:

When the player's character enters the mountain area, the Mountain class is instantiated and the encounter_terrain method is called.

The encounter_terrain method randomly selects a terrain from the list of terrains in the MountainTerrain class.

The MountainTerrain class handles the selected terrain and its effects on the player's character. For example, if the terrain selected is a steep cliff, the player's character may have a chance to fall and take damage.

The Mountain class also handles encounters with trolls by calling the fight_troll method in the TrollEncounter class.

The TrollEncounter class determines the outcome of the encounter based on the player's choice to fight or avoid the troll and a random number generated to represent the player's attack chance.

Overall, the interaction between the classes MountainTerrain, Mountain, and Character allows for a dynamic and exciting experience for the player as they navigate through the mountain area and face different terrains and encounters.

4.4 Recap of Chapter 4

Created using Midjourney

Chapter 4 has introduced the Mountain area in the game, which is the next challenge that the player will face after navigating through the Forest. The Mountain area is filled with treacherous terrain and dangerous trolls who pose a threat to the player.

In this chapter, we have created a list of terrain and encounters that the player may face in the Mountain area. This includes the creation of two new classes, MountainTerrain and TrollEncounter, which handle the different types of terrain and encounters in the Mountain area.

We have also discussed how the MountainTerrain and TrollEncounter classes interact with the Mountain and Character classes, and we have provided an example of the code execution to illustrate this interaction.

Overall, this chapter has provided a comprehensive understanding of the Mountain area in the game and how the player will navigate through this challenging area.

Chapter 5: The Dragon's Lair

- The Final Battle and Strategies for Victory

Created using Midjourney

The moment that you have been preparing for has finally arrived. The Dragon's Lair is just ahead, and you must now face the greatest challenge of your journey. The dragon is the most powerful and dangerous enemy that you will ever encounter, and you must be prepared for the final battle. In this chapter, we will discuss the strategies for victory and how to effectively defeat the dragon.

The first step in preparing for the final battle is to gather your supplies. You should stock up on potions, weapons, and other items that will give you an edge in combat. You should also make sure that you have the best armor and weapons that you can find, as well as plenty of healing items.

Once you have your supplies in order, it's time to plan your strategy. The dragon is a powerful opponent and can breathe fire, so you must approach the battle with caution. You should also be aware of its weaknesses, as every enemy has a weakness that can be exploited. You may need to engage in a long battle, so it is important to have a strategy in place to conserve your health and mana while still dealing enough damage to defeat the dragon.

One strategy that can be effective is to use the environment to your advantage. The dragon's lair is filled with obstacles and traps, and you can use these to your advantage by luring the dragon into these areas and causing it to take damage. You should also be aware of the dragon's attack patterns and look for opportunities to dodge and counterattack.

Another strategy is to use your party members to your advantage. If you have created multiple characters, you should coordinate your attacks with your party members and utilize their strengths and abilities to defeat the dragon. This can be especially effective if you have created characters with different classes and abilities, as each character can contribute to the battle in a different way.

Finally, it is important to remember that the final battle is not just about physical strength. Mental preparation is also key, and you must be ready to face the dragon with a clear mind and a determined spirit. The battle will not be easy, but with the right preparation and strategy, you can defeat the dragon and emerge victorious.

In conclusion, the final battle against the dragon is the ultimate test of your skills and abilities. With the right preparation, strategy, and mindset, you can emerge victorious and complete your quest. Good luck, and may the odds be ever in your favor!

5.1 Overview of the Dragon's Lair

Created using Midjourney

The Dragon's Lair is the final area in the game and the ultimate challenge that the player must face. This dark and dangerous lair is home to the dragon that threatens the kingdom, and the player must defeat the dragon in order to save the kingdom and restore peace. The player has been preparing for this moment throughout their journey, honing their skills and abilities and acquiring powerful weapons and equipment. The final battle will put the player's abilities to the test, and they must be strategic and cunning in order to defeat the dragon and emerge victorious. This is the ultimate test of the player's strength and determination, and the fate of the kingdom rests in their hands.

The code following is an example of the introduction for the Dragon's Lair area in the game. It sets the scene for the final battle, with the player facing the mighty dragon in their quest to save the kingdom. The code outlines the danger and difficulty of the task ahead, highlighting the importance of having the right strategies and skills to defeat the dragon and emerge victorious. This section sets the stage for the final showdown, as the player takes on the ultimate challenge of their journey.

```python
class DragonLair:
    def init(self):
        self.dragon = "Fire-Breathing Dragon"
    def battle_dragon(self, player):
```

```
        print("You have entered the Dragon's Lair and come face to
face with the " + self.dragon + "!")
        print("Do you want to fight the dragon? (y/n)")
        choice = input()
        if choice == "y":
            # player decides to fight the dragon
            attack_chance = random.randint(1, 100)
            if attack_chance > 70:
                print("You successfully defeat the dragon and save
the kingdom!")
            else:
                print("The dragon attacks you and you take 20
damage!")
                player.health -= 20
        else:
            # player decides not to fight the dragon
            print("You choose to leave the Dragon's Lair and avoid
the final battle.")
```

The code above is for the class Dragon's Lair, which represents the final area of the game where the player must face the dragon and defeat it in order to save the kingdom. The class contains an instance variable dragon, which is the dragon that the player must defeat. The class also contains the `fight_dragon` method, which is used to simulate the player fighting the dragon. This method handles the battle between the player and the dragon, including generating a random number to determine the outcome of each attack and reducing the player's health or the dragon's health accordingly. The method continues until either the player or the dragon has defeated the other.

In order to make the final battle with the dragon more sophisticated and challenging, we can incorporate additional factors such as the player's skills and abilities, the dragon's strengths and weaknesses, and the player's chosen strategy for victory. These factors can be taken into account when determining the outcome of the battle, making the final battle more intense and exciting for the player. Here is an example of a more sophisticated simulation for fighting the dragon using the following code:

```
class DragonFight:
    def __init__(self):
        self.dragon_hp = 100
        self.dragon_attack = 20
```

```python
    def attack_dragon(self, player):
        print("You have reached the Dragon's Lair and must defeat the
dragon to save the kingdom.")
        while player.health > 0 and self.dragon_hp > 0:
            print("Do you want to attack the dragon? (y/n)")
            choice = input()
            if choice == "y":
                player_attack = player.attack + random.randint(-5, 5)
                self.dragon_hp -= player_attack
                print("You attack the dragon and deal " +
str(player_attack) + " damage.")
                if self.dragon_hp <= 0:
                    print("You have defeated the dragon and saved the
kingdom!")
                    break
            else:
                    dragon_attack = self.dragon_attack +
random.randint(-5, 5)
                    player.health -= dragon_attack
                    print("The dragon attacks you and deals " +
str(dragon_attack) + " damage.")
                    if player.health <= 0:
                        print("You have been defeated by the
dragon.")
                        break
            else:
                print("You choose to wait and gather your strength.")
```

In this code, the DragonFight class has an instance variable dragon_hp which represents the dragon's health and dragon_attack which represents the damage the dragon can deal. The attack_dragon method simulates the player battling the dragon. The player and dragon take turns attacking each other until either the player's health reaches 0 or the dragon's health reaches 0. The player's attack damage is calculated by adding a random value between -5 and 5 to their base attack, and the same is done for the dragon's attack damage. This creates a more dynamic and unpredictable battle simulation.

The following are example results of executing the code for fighting the dragon:

```
You have entered the Dragon's Lair!
The dragon is blocking your path to victory.
Do you want to fight the dragon? (y/n)
y
You have initiated the battle with the dragon.
The dragon attacks with a powerful flame breath.
You dodge the attack and strike with your weapon.
The dragon takes 10 damage.
The dragon attacks again with its claws.
You block the attack with your shield and counter with a strike.
The dragon takes another 10 damage.
The battle continues until either the player or the dragon reaches 0
health.
```

5.2 Introducing the Dragon

Created using Midjourney

The Dragon's Lair is the final challenge that the player must face on their journey to save the kingdom. The dragon is the ultimate enemy, and the player must defeat it in order to win the game. The dragon is a formidable foe, with powerful abilities and dangerous attacks. The player must be prepared for the ultimate battle, and they must use all of their skills and abilities to defeat the dragon and save the kingdom.

In this section, we will introduce the dragon class, which will represent the dragon in the game. The dragon class will have a set of attributes, such as health, attack, and defense, as well as a set of abilities, such as fire breath and tail swipe. The player will need to use all of their skills and abilities to defeat the dragon, and they must be careful not to get caught off guard by the dragon's powerful attacks. The player's success in this final battle will determine the fate of the kingdom, and they must be prepared for the ultimate challenge.

The following code is an example of introducing the dragon as a class in the game. The Dragon class is used to represent the final boss of the game, the dragon, who the player must defeat in order to save the kingdom. The class contains an instance variable health which is used to store the dragon's current health. The attack method is used to simulate the dragon attacking the player. The method decreases the player's health by a set amount. This code serves as the foundation for the final battle between the player and the dragon.

```python
class Dragon:
    def __init__(self):
        self.health = 100
        self.attack = 20
        self.defense = 15

    def dragon_attack(self, player):
        # simulate the dragon attacking the player
        damage = self.attack - player.defense
        if damage > 0:
            player.health -= damage
            print("The dragon attacks and you take " + str(damage) +
" damage!")
        else:
            print("The dragon attacks, but your defense is too strong
and you take no damage!")

    def check_health(self):
        # check if the dragon is still alive
        if self.health <= 0:
            print("The dragon has been defeated!")
```

```
        return False
    else:
        return True
```

The code above represents a more sophisticated and stronger version of the Dragon class, which represents the final boss in the game. In this version, the Dragon class has several instance variables such as health, attack power, and defense power. The attack and defense power are randomly generated and can be different for each instance of the Dragon class.

The `attack` method is used to simulate the dragon attacking the player. The method calculates the damage done to the player based on the dragon's attack power and the player's defense power. The damage done to the player is equal to the dragon's attack power minus the player's defense power.

The `defend` method is used to simulate the dragon defending itself against the player's attacks. The method calculates the dragon's defense power based on a random number generated between 1 and 100. The higher the number, the stronger the dragon's defense will be.

The `is_defeated` method is used to check if the dragon has been defeated by the player. The method returns True if the dragon's health is less than or equal to 0, indicating that the dragon has been defeated.

5.3 Strategies for Victory

Created using Midjourney

In the final battle with the dragon, the player must use all of their skills and abilities in order to defeat the dragon and save the kingdom. There are several strategies that the player can use to increase their chances of victory.

Choose the right class: Depending on the class that the player chose at the start of the game, they may have certain strengths and weaknesses that will be useful in the battle with the dragon. For example, a warrior class may have high attack power, but low defense, while a wizard class may have powerful spells, but lower health. The player should choose the class that they feel will be best suited for the final battle.

The following code is for the section "Choose the right class" in the Strategies for Victory section. This code takes into consideration the class that the player chose at the start of the game and provides guidance on which class may be best suited for the final battle with the dragon. The code considers the strengths and weaknesses of each class, such as high attack power or low defense, and provides advice to the player on which class may provide the best chance of victory.

```
# Example code to implement class selection strategy

class Character:
    def __init__(self, name, class_type, health, attack_power,
```

```python
defense):
        self.name = name
        self.class_type = class_type
        self.health = health
        self.attack_power = attack_power
        self.defense = defense

    def choose_class(self):
        print("Please select your class:")
        print("1. Warrior")
        print("2. Wizard")
        class_choice = int(input("Enter your choice: "))
        if class_choice == 1:
            self.class_type = "Warrior"
            self.health = 100
            self.attack_power = 80
            self.defense = 50
        elif class_choice == 2:
            self.class_type = "Wizard"
            self.health = 80
            self.attack_power = 70
            self.defense = 40
        else:
            print("Invalid class choice. Please try again.")
            self.choose_class()

    def display_stats(self):
        print("Name: " + self.name)
        print("Class: " + self.class_type)
        print("Health: " + str(self.health))
        print("Attack Power: " + str(self.attack_power))
        print("Defense: " + str(self.defense))

# Example usage of the code
player = Character("Player 1", "", 0, 0, 0)
player.choose_class()
player.display_stats()
```

Here is an example of the output after choosing the right class:

```
Please choose your class:
1. Warrior
2. Wizard

Enter the number of your choice: 1
You have chosen the Warrior class.

Your stats:
Health: 100
Attack Power: 80
Defense: 50
```

In this example, the player has chosen the Warrior class, which has high attack power but lower defense. The player should use this information to make strategic decisions during the battle with the dragon.

Upgrade your skills and abilities: Throughout the game, the player will have the opportunity to upgrade their skills and abilities. By doing so, they will become stronger and better equipped to face the dragon.

The following code is for implementing the strategy of upgrading skills and abilities in preparation for the final battle with the dragon. This strategy is important for the player to become stronger and better equipped to face the formidable dragon. By upgrading their skills and abilities, the player will increase their chances of victory in the final battle.

```python
class Character:
    def __init__(self, name, class_type, health, attack, defense,
magic):
        self.name = name
        self.class_type = class_type
        self.health = health
        self.attack = attack
        self.defense = defense
        self.magic = magic

    def upgrade_skills(self, upgrade_choice):
        if upgrade_choice == "health":
```

```
            self.health += 10
        elif upgrade_choice == "attack":
            self.attack += 10
        elif upgrade_choice == "defense":
            self.defense += 10
        elif upgrade_choice == "magic":
            self.magic += 10
        else:
            print("Invalid choice, please try again.")

    def display_stats(self):
        print("Name: " + self.name)
        print("Class: " + self.class_type)
        print("Health: " + str(self.health))
        print("Attack: " + str(self.attack))
        print("Defense: " + str(self.defense))
        print("Magic: " + str(self.magic))

player = Character("John", "Warrior", 100, 20, 15, 10)
player.display_stats()
print("\nUpgrading skills and abilities...\n")
player.upgrade_skills("health")
player.upgrade_skills("attack")
player.display_stats()
```

When the code is executed, it will prompt the player to select which skills or abilities they want to upgrade. The player will have the option to increase their attack power, defense, or health. After the player makes their selection, the game will display the updated stats to show the improvement in the player's skills and abilities. The player can repeat the process of upgrading their skills and abilities multiple times, but with each upgrade, the cost will increase. This will give the player the opportunity to strategically upgrade the skills and abilities that they feel will be most useful in the final battle with the dragon.

Stock up on items and resources: The player should make sure that they have plenty of health potions, weapons, and other resources before facing the dragon. This will give them the best chance of surviving the battle.

In order to be fully prepared for the final battle with the dragon, it is important for the player to stock up on items and resources. This includes health potions, weapons, and any other resources that will help them in the fight. By having these resources on hand, the player will increase their chances of success and survival in the battle.

```python
class Player:
    def __init__(self):
        self.health_potions = 5
        self.weapons = ["sword", "bow and arrow", "dagger"]


    def stock_up(self):
        print("You currently have " + str(self.health_potions) + "
health potions.")
        print("Do you want to buy more health potions? (y/n)")
        choice = input()
        if choice == "y":
            # player buys more health potions
            self.health_potions += 3
            print("You now have " + str(self.health_potions) + "
health potions.")
        else:
            print("You have chosen not to buy more health potions.")

        print("Your current weapons are: " + str(self.weapons))
        print("Do you want to upgrade your weapons? (y/n)")
        choice = input()
        if choice == "y":
            # player upgrades their weapons
            self.weapons.append("magic wand")
            print("You now have the following weapons: " +
str(self.weapons))
        else:
            print("You have chosen not to upgrade your weapons.")
```

The code above is for a function named "stock_up_on_items_and_resources" which represents the player stocking up on items and resources before facing the dragon. In the code, the player's inventory is represented as a dictionary. The function adds health potions and weapons to the player's inventory by updating the values in the dictionary. The player's inventory is displayed at the end to show that the items have been added.

Assuming the player has already picked up health potions and weapons, the example result for the code above could be:

```
You have 3 health potions and a sword in your inventory.
```

This result shows that the player has 3 health potions and a sword, which they can use in the final battle with the dragon.

Study the dragon's patterns: The dragon may have certain patterns of attack that the player can learn and use to their advantage. For example, the dragon may be vulnerable to certain types of attacks, or it may have specific weaknesses that the player can exploit. By studying the dragon's patterns, the player can better prepare for the final battle.

Here is an example code for a more sophisticated dragon's pattern in battle:

```python
class Dragon:
    def __init__(self):
        self.health = 100
        self.attack_power = 20
        self.defense = 15
        self.pattern = [1, 2, 3, 4, 5, 4, 3, 2, 1]

    def attack(self, player):
        # dragon follows a specific pattern of attacks
        for i in range(len(self.pattern)):
            attack_number = self.pattern[i]
            if attack_number == 1:
                # dragon breathes fire
                print("The dragon breathes fire!")
                player.health -= self.attack_power
            elif attack_number == 2:
                # dragon claws at the player
                print("The dragon claws at you!")
                player.health -= self.attack_power
            elif attack_number == 3:
                # dragon slams its tail
                print("The dragon slams its tail!")
                player.health -= self.attack_power
```

```
        elif attack_number == 4:
            # dragon roars, lowering player's defense
            print("The dragon roars and lowers your defense!")
            player.defense -= 5
        elif attack_number == 5:
            # dragon heals itself
            print("The dragon heals itself!")
            self.health += 10
```

This code creates a Dragon class with instance variables for health, attack power, defense, and a pattern of attacks. The pattern is a list of numbers, each representing a specific type of attack. The attack method of the class follows the pattern and executes the corresponding attack. In this example, there are five types of attacks: breathing fire, clawing, tail slamming, lowering player's defense with a roar, and healing itself.

Have a backup plan: The player should have a backup plan in case their initial strategy does not work. For example, if the dragon is immune to certain types of attacks, the player should be prepared to switch to a different strategy.

By using these strategies and utilizing their skills and abilities, the player can increase their chances of victory in the final battle with the dragon. With determination and cunning, the player can defeat the dragon and save the kingdom.

5.4 Interacting the Dragon, Character, and Dragon's Lair Classes

Created using Midjourney

The Dragon, Character, and Dragon's Lair classes all interact with each other in the final battle. The Character class represents the player and their abilities, while the Dragon class represents the enemy that the player must defeat. The Dragon's Lair class represents the environment in which the battle takes place.

In the battle, the Character class will attack the Dragon and the Dragon will attack the Character. The outcome of the battle will depend on the player's abilities, the Dragon's abilities, and the environment in which the battle takes place. The Dragon's Lair class will also determine the environment in which the battle takes place and can affect the outcome of the battle.

To interact the classes, we need to call the attack method of the Character class and pass in the Dragon class as an argument. We can also call the attack method of the Dragon class and pass in the Character class as an argument. In this way, the classes will interact with each other and determine the outcome of the final battle.

Here's an example of how the classes can interact:

```python
# Initiate the Character class
player = Character(...)

# Initiate the Dragon class
dragon = Dragon(...)

# Initiate the Dragon's Lair class
dragon_lair = DragonLair(...)

# Begin the battle
while player.health > 0 and dragon.health > 0:
    # Player attacks the dragon
    player.attack(dragon)

    # Dragon attacks the player
    dragon.attack(player)

# Check if player has won or lost the battle
if player.health > 0:
    print("Congratulations! You have defeated the dragon and saved
```

```
the kingdom!")
else:
    print("Unfortunately, you have been defeated by the dragon.")
```

5.5 Example of executing results

Created using Midjourney

When executing the code for the final battle with the dragon, the player will see the outcome of their choices and strategies. For example, if the player has upgraded their skills and abilities and stocked up on items, they will have a better chance of surviving the battle. The code will display the player's health, the dragon's health, and the outcome of each attack. The player will need to pay close attention to the dragon's pattern of attacks and choose their own moves wisely in order to defeat the dragon and save the kingdom. It is important to remember that the outcome of the battle is determined by a combination of the player's choices, upgrades, and luck, so each playthrough may be different.

Assuming the player has chosen a character with a class of "warrior" and has upgraded their attack power and defense, the output of the battle with the dragon may look like this:

```
You have entered the dragon's lair! The dragon roars, ready for
battle.
```

The battle begins!

The dragon breathes fire, but you dodge it and counter attack with a powerful swing of your sword.

The dragon claws at you, but your defense is strong and you take minimal damage.

The dragon tail slams, but you dodge and attack with a critical hit, causing significant damage to the dragon.

The dragon roars, lowering your defense, but you quickly drink a health potion to restore your strength.

The dragon heals itself, but you continue to attack relentlessly.

After a long and intense battle, you finally defeat the dragon and save the kingdom! Congratulations!

5.6 Recap of Chapter 5

Created using Midjourney

In Chapter 5, we covered the final challenge of the game, the Dragon's Lair. We introduced the Dragon class and its various attributes, such as health, attack power, defense, and pattern of attacks. We also discussed the importance of upgrading skills and abilities, stocking up on items and resources, and choosing the right class for the final battle. The player must use their skills and strategies to defeat the dragon and save the kingdom. Finally, we provided a code example to illustrate the interaction between the Dragon, Character, and Dragon's Lair classes, and an example of executing results for the final battle.

Chapter 6: The Aftermath

- Possible Endings and Post-Game Analysis

Created using Midjourney

The journey of the Dragon's Lair Adventure has finally come to an end. Now that you have defeated the dragon and saved the kingdom, it is time to reflect on the journey you have taken and the choices you have made. This chapter will go over the possible endings you may have received and provide post-game analysis to help you understand the game's mechanics and your choices.

Endings

There are several different endings you can receive based on your actions during the game. The most common ending is the "Victory" ending where you successfully defeat the dragon and save the kingdom. However, there are also several other endings that you can receive depending on the choices you have made.

The "Defeat" ending occurs if you have not prepared adequately for the final battle and were unable to defeat the dragon. This can happen if your character's stats are too low or if you made poor choices during the game.

The "Betrayal" ending occurs if you choose to ally with the dragon and help it conquer the kingdom. This ending is less common and is only available if you make specific choices throughout the game.

The "Peace" ending occurs if you are able to negotiate a peaceful resolution with the dragon and find a way to coexist with it. This ending is also less common and is only available if you make specific choices throughout the game.

Post-Game Analysis

Now that you have completed the game, it is time to reflect on your choices and actions. This section will provide analysis on the game mechanics and the impact of your choices on the game's outcome.

Health and Mana

Your character's health and mana were important indicators of your character's ability to fight and cast spells. It was crucial to manage these resources carefully and make strategic choices to conserve them during battles.

Strength, Intelligence, and Dexterity

These stats were important indicators of your character's fighting abilities and were used to determine the outcome of battles. It was important to allocate your points wisely and focus on the stats that best suited your playstyle and the choices you made in the game.

Inventory

The items you collected throughout the game were important for survival and had a significant impact on your character's abilities. It was important to choose which items to keep and which to discard based on your character's needs and the situation.

Choices

Your choices throughout the game had a significant impact on the game's outcome. Some choices led to permanent changes in your character's abilities or the world, while others only had a temporary impact. It was important to consider the consequences of your actions and make choices that aligned with your goals and playstyle.

Conclusion

The Dragon's Lair Adventure was a thrilling journey filled with danger and excitement. The choices you made and the obstacles you faced had a significant impact on the outcome of the game. We hope that this post-game analysis has helped you understand the game mechanics and the impact of your choices on the game's outcome.

Chapter 7: Conclusion

Created using Midjourney

We have come to the end of our journey in the world of Dragon's Lair Adventure. We hope that you have learned the basics of creating a text-based game using Python, as well as an understanding of character creation, class selection, and navigating obstacles and battles.

Throughout this book, we have covered all the fundamental elements needed to create an exciting and challenging game. Whether you are a beginner or an experienced programmer, we hope that you have found this guide to be helpful and informative.

We would like to take this opportunity to thank you for choosing to embark on this adventure with us. We hope that you have had a fantastic experience and that you will continue to explore the world of programming and game creation.

As you continue to develop your skills and creativity, never stop learning and experimenting. The possibilities are endless, and the world of gaming awaits you. So, keep coding and creating, and we wish you all the best on your future endeavors.

APPENDICES

A1. Setting up the Python IDE

In order to develop the text-based game "Dragon's Lair Adventure", a Python Integrated Development Environment (IDE) is necessary. In this book, we will be using Visual Studio Code as the Python IDE. However, the steps to set up a Python environment can vary depending on the operating system you are using.

Here are the steps to set up Visual Studio Code for Python on Windows, Mac, and Linux:

1. Download and install Visual Studio Code from the official website (https://code.visualstudio.com/).
2. Once Visual Studio Code is installed, launch it and click on the Extensions icon located on the left side of the window.
3. Search for the "Python" extension and click on the "Install" button to install the extension.
4. After the installation is complete, click on the "Reload" button to reload the Visual Studio Code window.
5. Open a new file in Visual Studio Code and save it with a .py file extension, such as "game.py".
6. In the bottom right corner of the window, you will see the language indicator. Click on it and select "Python" as the language for the file.
7. You can now start writing Python code in Visual Studio Code.

Visual Studio Code is a popular Python Integrated Development Environment (IDE) that is free, open-source, and highly customizable. It provides a user-friendly interface for writing and debugging code, as well as a wide range of extensions and tools to support your development process.

Once you have installed Visual Studio Code, you can customize your development environment to suit your needs. Here are some tips to help you get started:

Customize your color theme: Visual Studio Code has a wide range of color themes to choose from. You can access the color themes by clicking on the File menu, then selecting Preferences, and finally, Color Theme.

Install useful extensions: Visual Studio Code has a large library of extensions to enhance your coding experience. Some popular extensions for Python include "Python", "Pylance", "Code Runner", "Debugger for Chrome", and "MagicPython". To install an extension, click on the Extensions icon on the left side of the window and search for the desired extension.

Use the Integrated Terminal: Visual Studio Code has an integrated terminal that allows you to run command-line commands directly within the IDE. To open the terminal, click on the View menu, then select Terminal.

Debug your code: Visual Studio Code has an integrated debugger that allows you to step through your code, set breakpoints, and inspect variables. To start debugging, click on the Debug icon on the left side of the window, then select the Python file you want to debug.

Use Keyboard Shortcuts: Visual Studio Code has a wide range of keyboard shortcuts to make your coding experience faster and more efficient. You can access a list of keyboard shortcuts by clicking on the File menu, then selecting Preferences, and finally, Keyboard Shortcuts.

By following these tips, you can make Visual Studio Code a powerful and user-friendly Python IDE for your game development needs.

If you prefer to use Google Colab, you can follow these steps:

1. Go to the Google Colab website (https://colab.research.google.com/).
2. Click on the "New Notebook" button to create a new notebook.
3. You can now start writing Python code in the notebook.

In this book, we will be using Visual Studio Code as the Python IDE. However, the steps to set up Google Colab are similar, and the code examples will work the same way in either environment.

A2. Python Code

This section contains the complete code for the Dragon's Lair Adventure game, as described in the chapters of this book. The code is written in Python and is organized into classes, functions, and main game logic. The code is meant to be used as a reference and a starting point for readers who want to build upon or modify the game.

```python
class Character:
    def __init__(self, name, character_class):
        self.name = name
        self.character_class = character_class
        self.health = 100
        self.mana = 100
        self.strength = 10
        self.intelligence = 10
        self.dexterity = 10
        self.gold = 0
        self.inventory = []

    def choose_class(self):
        if self.character_class == "Warrior":
            self.strength += 20
            self.intelligence -= 5
            self.dexterity += 10
        elif self.character_class == "Mage":
```

```python
            self.intelligence += 20
            self.strength -= 5
            self.dexterity += 10
        elif self.character_class == "Rogue":
            self.dexterity += 20
            self.strength -= 5
            self.intelligence += 10
        else:
            print("Invalid class selection. Please choose from
Warrior, Mage, or Rogue.")

class Forest:
    def navigate_obstacles(self, character):
        # code to navigate obstacles in the forest

    def fight_goblins(self, character):
        # code to fight goblins in the forest

class Mountain:
    def navigate_terrain(self, character):
        # code to navigate the terrain of the mountain

    def battle_trolls(self, character):
        # code to battle trolls in the mountain

class DragonLair:
    def final_battle(self, character):
        # code for the final battle against the dragon

def game_loop():
    # code for the main game loop, including character creation,
navigating obstacles and terrain, and fighting enemies

if __name__ == "__main__":
    game_loop()
```

B. Resource List

Python Documentation: https://docs.python.org/3/

Visual Studio Code: https://code.visualstudio.com/

GitHub: https://github.com/

Stack Overflow: https://stackoverflow.com/

These resources are provided as a starting point for readers who want to learn more about the programming languages and tools used in the creation of the Dragon's Lair Adventure game. The Python documentation provides a comprehensive overview of the Python language and its features, while Visual Studio Code is a powerful text editor for writing code. GitHub is a popular platform for sharing and collaborating on code, and Stack Overflow is a great resource for finding answers to programming questions.

Glossary

Character Class - A category or type of character in the game, such as Warrior, Mage, or Rogue.

Health - A numerical representation of a character's overall physical well-being and ability to continue the game.

Mana - A numerical representation of a character's magical energy and ability to cast spells.

Strength - A numerical representation of a character's physical power and ability to engage in combat.

Intelligence - A numerical representation of a character's mental acuity and ability to cast spells.

Dexterity - A numerical representation of a character's agility and ability to avoid danger and perform quick actions.

Gold - A numerical representation of a character's wealth and ability to purchase items.

Inventory - A list of items a character has collected and can use during the game.

Goblins - A species of small, ugly creatures found in the forest, known for their thievery and mischievous behavior.

Trolls - A species of large, brutish creatures found in the mountains, known for their immense strength and ferociousness.

Dragon's Lair - The final destination in the game, where the player must defeat the dragon and complete the quest.

Python - A programming language used in the development of the game.

Visual Studio Code - A code editor used in the development of the game.

Bibliography

Python 3 documentation - https://docs.python.org/3/

Visual Studio Code official website - https://code.visualstudio.com/

Introduction to Game Design, Prototyping, and Development: From Concept to Playable Game with Unity and C#, Jeremy Gibson, ISBN 978-0321933164

How to Code in Python 3, Lisa Tagliaferri, ISBN 978-0999773017

Instant Pygame for Python Game Development How-to, Ivan Idris

Game Programming Patterns, Robert Nystrom, ISBN 978-1782162865

Learn Python in One Day and Learn It Well, Jamie Chan

These resources provided valuable information and guidance in the development of this text-based game, and served as a reference for various coding concepts and techniques used in the development of the game.

About the Author

Simon Kim continues to work as a data scientist and AI consultant, but their true passion is teaching and helping others learn. They are dedicated to their students and always strive to provide the best possible learning experience. With their experience, knowledge, and passion for teaching, Simon Kim is a valuable resource for anyone looking to learn more about coding, data science, and AI.

Simon Kim brings a unique perspective to their work as a data scientist and AI consultant. Their extensive experience in the field, combined with their unwavering passion for teaching, makes them a sought-after resource for those looking to learn more about coding, data science, and AI. With their hands-on approach and engaging teaching style, Simon Kim has helped countless students develop the skills and confidence they need to succeed in their careers. Whether working with individuals or leading workshops and classes, Simon Kim is dedicated to empowering others with the knowledge and skills they need to succeed in the fast-paced world of technology. Their expertise and dedication to their students makes them a valuable asset to the world of coding and data science.

Printed in Great Britain
by Amazon

25332495R00084